Two Colorado Odysseys

Two Colorado Odysseys

✦

Chief Ouray
Porter Nelson

Robert B. Houston, Jr.

iUniverse, Inc.
New York Lincoln Shanghai

Two Colorado Odysseys
Chief Ouray Porter Nelson

iUniverse books may be ordered through booksellers or by contacting:

iUniverse
2021 Pine Lake Road, Suite 100
Lincoln, NE 68512
www.iuniverse.com
1-800-Authors (1-800-288-4677)

ISBN-13: 978-0-595-35860-1 (pbk)
ISBN-13: 978-0-595-80318-7 (ebk)
ISBN-10: 0-595-35860-8 (pbk)
ISBN-10: 0-595-80318-0 (ebk)

Printed in the United States of America

Contents

Prologue

✦

The How and Why

Under the Freedom of Information Act, material which might reveal intelligence sources and methods is exempt from release. I am not going to claim that exemption here; I'm going to come clean up front. As the title to this book suggests, it deals with the activities in Colorado of two individuals. The two never met, indeed were never in Colorado at the same time. The first is Ute Chief Ouray, a historic figure. The second is my maternal grandfather, W. Porter Nelson, not a historic figure. Both were born outside Colorado, but in Colorado they had their moments in the sun. Both died in Colorado, but there the similarities end. My method of treating two disparate persons in one book is unusual, the first part dealing with the Colorado of the Indians, and the second with the Colorado of a white newcomer who lived in worked in the Colorado Ouray and his Utes left behind. The resulting two-barreled work does, I think, yield a broader understanding of Colorado history.

Chief Ouray's name is attached to a county in Colorado, to one town in Colorado and one town in Utah, as well as to a mountain in Colorado. Ouray was not thus richly honored for battles with whites, like Geronomo or Cochise of the Apaches, or Sitting Bull of the Sioux. No, Ouray is renowned for his role as a peacemaker. Several Ouray biographies have been written, but none by persons who knew Ouray personally. Much of their information came from persons who also had not known him. So in this book, I decided to focus on sources close to what actually happened. These were in the first place the many letters sent to the Commissioner of Indian Affairs in Washington, now on microfilm at the National Archives in Washington but surprisingly little tapped. The letters came mostly from persons on the front line of dealing with Ouray and his Tabeguache. A few came from citizens concerned about government failings in controlling the Indians. The microfilmed correspondence is voluminous. The researcher's task in dealing with this resource, as with most material, is to extract from a mass of

1

worthless rock those truly valuable items which provide insight into the motives and character of the main figures involved.

These first hard records of Ouray's rise from obscurity to leadership were created by the agents to the Tabeguache band of Utes. who dealt directly with him. All these agents are listed below with their appointment dates,[1] whether at Conejos or the later locations of the Tabeguache agency.

Agent	Date of Appointment
Lafayette Head	June 27, 1860
Lt. Calvin Speer	June 26, 1869
Jabez Nelson Trask	February 18, 1871
Charles Adams	May 28, 1872
Henry F. Bond	May 20, 1874
Willard D. Wheeler	September 14, 1876
Joseph B. Abbott	December 3, 1877
Leverett M. Kelly	September 24, 1878
Wilson M. Stanley	April 28, 1879
George Sherman, Acting	January 1, 1880
William H. Berry	April 22, 1880

The first four agents watched Ouray's rise to the position of head chief, the remaining agents dealt with Ouray when he was trying to fulfill that role. Arguably, the best of these agents were the first and longest serving, Lafayette Head, later a Lieutenant Governor of Colorado, and the third, Charles Adams. Each had established himself in the West well before being appointed agent, and thus neither was a "greenhorn" when named agent.

Indian agents and complaining citizens were not the only creators of official records on Ouray. Territorial Governors of Colorado before 1870 also knew Ouray, since until1870, these Governors served also as *ex officio* Superintendents of Indian Affairs in Colorado.

---

1.   Edward E. Hill, _The Office of Indian Affairs, 1824-1880: History and Sketches_, Clearwater Publishing Co. N. Y., 1974. p. 40-42

Governor	Date of Appointment
William Gilpin	March 25, 1861
John Evans	March 26, 1862
Alexander Cumming	October 21, 1865
A. Cameron Hunt	May 10, 1867
Edward M. McCook	April 17, 1869

Chairman of the Board of Indian Commissioners, the Felix R. Brunot who in 1873 proposed Ouray as "head chief of the Confederated Utes," also enriched our knowledge of Ouray through his reports. The Secretary of the Interior under President Rutherford B. Hayes, German immigrant Carl Schurz, had personal contact with Ouray when the latter visited Washington and left valuable impressions. Quartermaster General James Rusling, who went with Governor Cumming in 1866 on visits to the Utes, wrote of his encounters with Ouray in a book published in 1874. C. W. Jocknick, sent to Los Pinos from Washington in 1872 to look into the problems of agent Trask, sent Washington valuable reports not only on the Agency, but also covering Ouray. In addition, one private party left a valuable, almost contemporary account of Ouray. This was Sidney Jocknick, probably the son of the Inspector of 1872. Sidney Jocknick first came to the Los Pinos agency in 1871 under agent Trask, and then served as a cattle herder under agents Adams, Bond and Wheeler. His jobs at Los Pinos were menial, but Sidney Jocknick was a good observer and reporter. His book, although appearing in print only years later, is nonetheless a valuable contribution to our knowledge of Ouray and his rise to the top.[2] Such were my sources.

Public knowledge of Ouray regrettably was left poorer by the failure of Russian immigrant and entrepreneur extraordinary Otto Mears to leave anything in writing about the Chief. Mears' contacts with Ouray extended over a longer period than those of any other white person, inside or outside the Government. Mears evidently could make himself understood in the Ute language. Mears for a time was a business partner of Tabeguache Agent Lafayette Head at Conejos, and transferred his business operations to Saguache when the Tabeguache Agency moved north. He continued to be a supplier to the agency when it moved westward, and attended many Ute negotiations. He also built roads to and through

---

2.   Sidney Jocknick, *Early Days on the Western Slope of Colorado*, Western Reflections, Ouray, Col., 1998.

the Ute Reservation. A joint photograph of Mears and Ouray in 1870 testifies to Mears' close relations with Ouray. Mears might have added to our knowledge of Ouray's first wife, the mother of his only child who was lost to hostile Indians. Mears might also have given us more insights into Ouray's second wife, the famous Chipeta. Chipeta was important as Ouray's primary confidante, who went with him to Washington on several occasions. Chipeta survived Ouray by many years, and although banished to Utah in 1881 with all the Tabeguache, became famous in her own right after Ouray's death.

The second individual I cover in this book is my maternal grandfather, William Porter Nelson, who took up residence in Colorado only in 1888, well after Ouray's death. I published a chronology of Nelson's life in 1997,[3] the centenary of his election as Mayor of Aspen. In writing that chronology, my method was to draw on family sources, supplemented by the sporadic coverage of him in contemporary Aspen newspapers. This produced a book of "Just the bare facts, Ma'am!"genre. In my current book, I have gone to more varied sources, all primary because, apart from my 1997 book, no one else has written anything about Porter Nelson. Not a history-changing figure like Chief Ouray, Nelson led a life not atypical of what a number of Coloradans of the last part of the 19th century and the first part of the 20th lived through. I include Nelson's Colorado odyssey in this book in the belief that "ontogeny recapitulates biogeny."

There was a time in the history of the cinematographic industry in the United States when theater owners felt that the best way to get the public to buy tickets and come inside was to offer them a "double feature," two feature films for the price of one. The same line of thought has underlain the design of this book.

---

3.   Robert B. Houston, Jr., *The Battle over Silver: Porter Nelson in Aspen*, Professional Press, Chapel Hill, N. C., 1997.

PART I
Chief Ouray

Library of Congress

1

Written Records Begin of Chief Ouray

In a sense, the Ute Indians were the original owners of much of Colorado. Long before the White Man came to mark boundaries, Utes roamed in what became Colorado, northern New Mexico and in Utah. In time, the United States came to recognize seven different bands of Utes in Colorado and New Mexico.[1] The Tabeguache band was the largest of these seven. The Tabeguache, in 1860, were the first Utes to be given an agency in what became Colorado in 1861, set up near the largely Mexican town of Conejos. In 1863, the Tabeguache also became the first Colorado Utes to sign a treaty with the United States ceding title to land. It was at Conejos where the first written records of Ouray came into being, although important records of Ouray were created later at the other locations of the Tabeguache agency.

To cover Ouray's poorly documented early formative years, several biographies are available. The biographers generally agree that Ouray was born near Taos, New Mexico, around 1833. His mother, who died while Ouray was still young, is said to have been a Tabeguache Ute. His father had been raised by the Jicarilla Apaches, but may have been a Ute captured in battle as a child by those Apaches.[2] Some speculate that Ouray may have had some schooling with Catholic friars at Taos.[3] Biog-

---

1. None of the old band names are in use today. The Uintah, Grand River and Yampa bands were collectively called the White Rivers for a time. After they and the Tabeguache were sent to join other Utes already established on a reservation in Utah, they all became known as the Northern Utes. The Muache and Capote bands, originally roaming mostly in New Mexico, are now known as the Southern Utes with a reservation based at Ignacio, Colorado. The Wiminuches are now known as the Mountain Utes, with a reservation based at Towoac, Colorado.

2. Fullest account in P. David Smith, *Ouray, Chief of the Utes*, Wayfarer Press, Ouray, CO, 1986, p. 34, but the facts are also on the Southern Ute Web Site.

3. Smith, *op. cit.*, p. 35

raphers agree that Ouray remained for some years near Taos, where he and a younger brother worked for (and may have lived with) a Mexican family, herding sheep, chopping wood and doing other household chores.[4] His early life was thus centered in a mostly Mexican environment, and was not that of a typical Ute child living in a nomadic family. This background helps explain Ouray's later role as an important link between Utes and whites, and his openness to adopting some "white ways."

Ouray probably did not leave the Taos area until about 1850 when biographers think he went to live with the Tabeguache.[5] He probably considered he belonged to the Tabeguache because his mother had been one. One biographer suggests Ouray in time attained stature among the Tabeguache as an "enforcer" among them for White River Ute Chief Nevava. Nevava apparently was accepted as chief by more than one band of Utes, with influence not only with the White Rivers but also with some Utes in Utah.[6] Ouray also may have won the confidence of the Tabeguache "war chief" at the time, Shavano. But Ouray was not yet the top Tabeguache.

Before Colorado Territory was established in 1861, the Tabeguache band had been the responsibility of the Superintendent of Indian Affairs in New Mexico. That Superintendent established an agency for the Tabeguache band on the Conejos River in 1860, following a suggestion made in 1856 by Kit Carson, then the Indian agent at Taos. The New Mexico Superintendent's reason for setting up the Conejos agency was to separate the Tabeguache from other Indians being served at the agency at Abiquiu, namely the Muache and Capote Utes.[7] Selecting Conejos as the base for the agency was a lazy man's decision. The person named as Tabeguache agent, Lafayette Head, was already established in business there and had his own warehouses. No need to erect expensive buildings for the agency. But setting up an agency at Conejos was a questionable idea. Since many Mexicans lived in the lower San Luis valley, no real separation between whites and Indians was achieved by putting the agency there. Conejos in fact was the site of the first permanent church in what later became Colorado, built in 1858.

---

4.   Nancy C. Wood, _When Buffalo Free the Mountains_, Doubleday & Co., Garden City, N. Y, 1980, p. 13.
5.   Smith, _op. cit._, p. 43.
6.   Virginia M. Simmons, _The Ute Indians of Utah, Colorado and New Mexico_, Boulder, University Press of Colorado, 2000, p. 126. On the other hand, the Southern Ute listing of all historical Ute leaders does mention Nevava.
7.   Annual Report of the Commissioner of Indian Affairs (hereafter CIA), 1860, p. 162.

The first church in Colorado was built on this Conejos site in 1858, before the Tabeguache Agency came here.

The New Mexico move to separate the various bands of Utes ran counter to later Colorado efforts to consolidate all the Utes in one reservation, or in two adjoining reservations, served by as few agents as possible. The Colorado authorities did not like having an agency in the midst of Mexican settlements, occupying land which white newcomers might soon want to take up. While the Tabeguache were nomadic and did not reside permanently at their agency, they did come there frequently, and viewed the agency as the main source of goods from the government. After assuming responsibility for the Conejos Agency, the Colorado authorities decided to schedule the periodic distribution of goods well away from Conejos[8] so as to avoid

8.   Letter Gov. Evans to the CIA, July 6, 1865, Roll 198, NARA Microfilm Publication M234, Letters Received, Office of Indian Affairs, Washington D.C. (Hereafter simply NARA M234).

attracting the Tabeguache into the area of Mexican settlements. The authorities feared, as in fact happened, that difficulties might arise between the local Mexicans and the Tabeguache.[9]

The Act of February 28, 1861[10] which gave birth to the Territory of Colorado brought the existing Conejos agency for the Tabeguache within the bounds of the new Territory, and the Colorado Territorial Governors were made *ex officio* Superintendents of Indian Affairs in Colorado. There is no evidence that Washington had been thinking of replacing Lafayette Head as Indian Agent at Conejos. But when Denver took over supervision of the Conejos Agency, Governor Gilpin recommended to Washington that Head be kept on. Gilpin described him as a good Republican, a supporter of the Lincoln Administration, fluent in Spanish and on good terms with Mexican population around Conejos.[11] Head would serve longer than anyone else as agent to the Tabeguache (1860-1868).

Head had to cope with perennial shortages of funds to operate the agency.[12] His stewardship would be attacked by such persons as Senator Charles Sumner (for allegedly paying the Tabeguache to free Navajo captives),[13] by some settlers near Conejos (for allegedly leading a mob to free a man from jail who was then tied to a tree and whipped),[14] and by the Commandant at nearby Fort Garland (for allegedly speculating in Government property).[15] Throughout, Head seems to have retained the confidence of his immediate supervisors, the various Colorado Territorial Governors, leaving his post as agent only when the time came to move the agency away from his base at Conejos. One Governor reported to Washington that Head was illiterate.[16] Illiterate or not, Lafayette Head was the person who oversaw creation of the first written records about Ouray.

When still only a territory, Colorado was represented in Congress by a single delegate in the House of Representatives. The delegate in 1862, Hiram Pitt Ben-

---

9.   Letter Gov. Evans to the CIA, July 9, 1865. Also, letter Gov. Evans to Major Lafayette Head, July 14, 1865, both Roll 198, NARA M234.
10. 12 Stat. 172
11. Letter Gov. Gilpin to the CIA, June 19, 1861, Roll 197, NARA M234.
12. Letter Gov. Gilpin to the acting CIA, February 18, 1862, and letter Gov. Evans to the CIA, August 6, 1862, both in Roll 197, NARA M234.
13. A cross reference sheet dated November 30, 1863 refers to the Sumner charges, Roll 197, NARA M234.
14. Letter from a Conejos resident to Gov. Evans, March 11, 1864, Roll 197, NARA M234.
15. Letter Major A. H. Meyers, Commandant at Fort Garland, to the Adjutant at Fort Leavenworth, August 28, 1862, Roll 197, NARA M234.
16. Letter Gov. Cumming to the CIA, August 28, 1862, Roll 198, NARA M234.

nett, wrote to the Commissioner of Indian Affairs urging the negotiation of treaties by which the Utes, and the more troublesome Plains Indians (Comanche,
Arapaho, Cheyenne, Kiowas), would vacate lands sought by the inflowing white
newcomers.[17] Also at this time, the General Land Office asked the Office of
Indian Affairs to extinguish Indian title to lands just east of the Rocky Mountains
so that it could carry out the surveys necessary for granting titles in this desirable
area to the incoming white farmers and ranchers.[18] The Secretary of Interior then
authorized the Office of Indian Affairs to bring a delegation of Indians to Washington, from both the Plains tribes and the Utes, with the goal of negotiating a
treaty by which the Indians would cede land.[19]

The Office of Indian Affairs told Lafayette Head to select members of a delegation to go to Washington in 1863, to include influential Utes from Conejos
and elsewhere. His choice of delegates was criticized by New Mexican officials.
One New Mexico official, claiming familiarity with the Indians at Conejos, said
that Head's group did not include real chiefs.[20] Head was also attacked by the
Commandant at Fort Garland, who tried to block Head and his Indians from
going to Washington. Head evaded this attempt.[21]

Since the Plains Indians and the Utes were nominally at war, the Utes could
not be put at risk while crossing the territory of their enemies, so measures had to
be taken to keep apart the Ute and Plains Indian delegations going to Washington. Colorado Governor John Evans secured a company of the U.S. Cavalry to
escort Head with his Ute delegation on the first leg of the trip to Washington.
They traveled along the Platte River from Denver to the railhead at St. Joseph,
Missouri.[22] Head included the young Ouray among the 13 Utes traveling with
him in February, 1863. One author asserts that when the Head delegation met
President Abraham Lincoln, Lincoln shook hands first with the young Ouray, a
chance gesture perhaps elevating Ouray in the eyes of his fellow Utes.[23]

---

17. Letter Colorado Delegate Bennett to the CIA, November 6, 1862, Roll 197, NARA M234.

18. Letter General Land Office to the CIA, April 26, 1861, Roll 197, NARA M234.

19. Letter Secretary of the Interior to the CIA, November 18, 1862, Roll 197, NARA M234.

20. Letter Superintendent of Indian Affairs of New Mexico to the CIA, February 21, 1863, Roll 197, NARA M234.

21. Letter Commandant at Fort Garland to the Adjutant at Fort Leavenworth, February 8, 1863, Roll 197, NARA M234.

22. Letter Gov. Evans to the CIA, February 3, 1863, Roll 197, NARA M234.

23. P. David Smith, *op cit*, p. 66.

In Washington, the Ute delegation apparently showed willingness to accept a reservation in return for a commitment on the part of the Government to pay the band $10,000 a year.[24] On the grounds that such things are important to an Indian, Head asked for seven silver medals to hand out later to selected Tabeguache.[25]

Since the Indian delegations in Washington had seemed favorably inclined towards a treaty, the Office of Indian Affairs appointed Colorado Territorial Governor Evans as head negotiator with them. Evans decided to negotiate first with the Plains Indians, and scheduled the Plains Indian talks for September 1, 1863. The negotiations with the Utes had to wait; these were set for Conejos on October 1, 1863. All the Ute bands, including those primarily roaming in New Mexico, were supposed to assemble at Conejos to negotiate a treaty by which all the Ute bands would agree to move to a single reservation in Colorado. Washington provided reinforcement for the talks by naming John Nicolay, from President Lincoln's hometown of Springfield, Illinois, as secretary of the negotiating team, and giving Nicolay $5,000 to pay negotiation expenses.[26] Evans asked for an additional $3,000 for the negotiation.[27] Some idea of how some of the money might be spent is shown by what Head on a later occasion informed Governor Cumming was needed for success in an Indian negotiation: 20 to 25 head of beef cattle, 50 head of sheep, 400-500 bushels of wheat, 12 bushels of sugar, and 10 sacks of coffee.[28]

The Superintendent of Indian Affairs in New Mexico helped in the October, 1863 Conejos talks by having two of his Indian Agents attend and bring representatives of the New Mexico Ute bands. Still Evans did not get the full participation that he had planned. While the Wiminuche band from New Mexico came, they declined to meet with the commission directly because of a recent attack upon them by the Cheyennes. The Grand River and Uintah bands did not come at all, having been found too late by the messenger sent out by their agent, Major Whiteley. Even with this reduced turnout, Evans encountered strong opposition to the idea of all the Ute bands moving to the reservation proposed in the valley of the San Juan River in the southwestern part of the Territory. In his report to Washington, Evans gave the following reasons for failure: (1) the agents for the Capote and Wiminuche bands, which bands claimed the San Juan valley,

24.   Telegram Head to the CIA, April 27, 1863, Roll 197, NARA M234.
25.   Letter Head to the CIA, March 6, 1862, Roll 197, NARA M234.
26.   Letter Nicolay to the CIA, July 24, 1863, Roll 197, NARA M234.
27.   Letter Gov. Evans to the CIA, August 26, 1863, Roll 197, NARA M234.
28.   Letter Gov. Cumming to the CIA, February 21, 1866, Roll 198, NARA M234.

said their Utes were not willing to give up their hunting grounds for this purpose; (2) these agents said their charges were satisfied with their current liberal treatment by the government and didn't want any change; (3) the agents doubted that the San Juan valley was large enough to accommodate all the bands; and (4) the Indians, when approached as a group, would entertain no proposition for any treaty whatsoever that would require them to settle down for the purpose of agriculture.[29]

Rather than accept total failure, Governor Evans decided to conclude a treaty with the Tabeguache alone. With some effort, Evans did get the Tabeguache to sign a treaty on October 7, 1863.[30] In his report to Washington, Governor Evans credited the good work of agent Head in bringing the Tabeguache delegation to Washington in the spring of 1863 for easing the way. After the Tabeguache signed the treaty, Secretary Nicolay distributed to selected chiefs and head men the seven silver medals that agent Head had requested long before and had picked up while in Washington,[31] and gave the chiefs certificates of their authority.[32]

From the point of view of the United States, the most important provisions of this treaty were these: the Tabeguache recognized the supremacy of the United States (Article 1); they accepted a reservation which, while large, was much smaller than the area they claimed as their traditional hunting grounds (Article 2); they agreed that the United States could establish military posts on this reservation, build roads and railroads through it, and that American citizens could conduct mining operations on it (Article 3). In view of the government's desire to settle all the Utes onto one reservation, the Tabeguache consent in Article 4 to having the Muache settle on their reservation is noteworthy. From the standpoint of the Tabeguache, the following provisions were most important: the U.S. agreed to pay them, every year for ten years, $10,000 worth of provisions and $10,000 worth of other goods (Article 8); for the purpose of improving the blood lines of their horses, the U.S. agreed to give the Tabeguache 5 good stallions in the year after treaty ratification (Article 9); and the U.S. agreed to supply a blacksmith, and also to give help to any Tabeguache household which takes up agriculture (Article 10).

Seen in the light of subsequent Ute treaties, the 1863 treaty is noteworthy for other reasons. First, it spelled out U.S. supremacy rather than assuming this as a given. Secondly, it described reservation boundaries in terms easily understand-

---

29.   CIA, 1863, p. 125.
30.   13 Stat. 673.
31.   Receipt signed by Head in Washington, April 22, 1863, Roll 197, NARA M234.
32.   CIA, 1863, p. 125.

able to the Indians, e. g. in terms of natural geographical features like a river source, or the summit of a range, rather than abstract terms of meridians of longitude or parallels of latitude, which would be difficult indeed for interpreters to explain to the Utes. Articles 9 and 10 of the 1863 treaty foretold more elaborate measures in later treaties encouraging the Utes to shift to an agricultural life style. The fact that Ouray was only the fourth Tabeguache recorded as signing the treaty at Conejos suggests he was not then considered by the band as their most influential leader.

Despite official praise for the 1863 treaty, the Senate, in ratifying it in March, 1864,[33] insisted on making revisions. The Senate wanted two major changes. One reduced the eastward extent of the Tabeguache reservation as delineated in Article 2. The other cut in half the annual government payment to Tabeguache provided in Article 10. So Governor Evans had to go back to the Indians to get them to accept Senate changes unfavorable to them. When Evans met with the Tabeguache, they objected particularly to the reservation boundary changes the Senate had made. The Indians maintained that the amputated reservation would not contain sufficient pasturage for their animals. After much discussion, Evans got nine Tabeguache chiefs and head men to mark their acceptance of the Senate changes, after the Governor persuaded the Grand River Utes to allow Tabeguache stock to be pastured in their lands. Evans also sweetened the deal by buying for immediate presentation to the Tabeguache two of the five fine American stallions promised them under Article 9 of the treaty.[34] Ouray was recorded as being the third Tabeguache to affix his X mark to this revised treaty. In 1864, Governor Evans had Ouray put on the payroll of the Conejos Agency as "interpreter." Ouray's salary in this position was $500 per year,[35] higher than the usual $400 paid to an interpreter.

Although proclaimed in force by President Lincoln on December 24, 1864, the treaty was never implemented, in the sense that the Tabeguache never moved to the reservation specified in the treaty, and the Government never paid them the annuities promised in the treaty. A. C. Hunt, who became Colorado Territorial Governor in May, 1867, questioned the wisdom of setting up a reservation for just one band of Utes. Hunt argued that "to remove one of these bands, and leave the other six to roam about among settlements, will not in the least remedy existing difficulties either among Indians or whites." The Interior Department

---

33.   13 Stat. 673.
34.   Letter from Gov. Evans, CIA, 1864, p. 223.
35.   Letter Evans to Head, July 14, 1865, NARA M234, Roll 198.

maintained that the reservation set up by the treaty of Oct. 7, 1863 was for the Tabeguache alone, and the Department could not force the other six bands, or any part of them, move there.[36] Even if the government dealt just with the Tabeguache, there were problems. Must the Tabeguache move away from their normal home base in the San Luis valley across the Continental Divide before the government took any steps to set up an agency there through which they could draw supplies? Could the Indians expect the government to build an agency way out in the wilderness before the Tabeguache took any steps to move there? Would the government have to defend the Tabeguache against attacks by the other bands? And if other Ute bands insisted on having their own reservations, comparable in size to the Tabeguache Reservation, how much of Colorado would be free of Indian claims? Limiting Indian land was an important goal. In 1863, the General Land Office proudly proclaimed that Indian title had been extinguished to one million acres of arable land in Colorado.[37]

Agent Head in 1865 recommended that the government place the Tabeguache on the reservation in charge of an agent, with United States troops in the vicinity, to maintain order and teach them the arts of husbandry.[38] Just before Governor Evans left office in that year, he tried to get the Tabeguache to move to the reservation provided in the 1863 treaty, and specifically to some spot near the Gunnison River. In one of his final letters as Governor written in September, 1865, Evans complained about the delay in getting the goods for distribution to the Tabeguache. Evans also explained how he had tried, but failed, to persuade a small group of Tabeguache Utes who were associated with the Grand River and Uintah Utes in the Middle Park to join the rest of the Tabeguache in South Park to receive their Government handouts.[39] The Ute bands were not close buddies.

Following Evans' failed efforts, and after Evans had left office, agent Head said that the Tabeguache wanted to send two chiefs to Washington to discuss moving to the reservation.[40] On taking office as Territorial Governor on October 21, 1865 as Evan's successor, Alexander Cumming discussed with Shavanavo, whom he described as the war chief of the Tabeguache and a brother-in-law of head chief Ouray, the Tabeguache desire for a new visit to Washington. Cumming persuaded Shavanavo to drop the idea of the Washington visit, and speculated

---

36. Report from the Secretary of Interior, Senate Executive Document 70 (40-2), Serial Set 1317.

37. Annual Report of the General Land Office, 1863, p. 18.

38. Letter Lafayette Head to Gov. Evans, August 10, 1865, CIA, 1865, p. 178.

39. Letter Gov. Evans to the CIA, Sept. 5, 1865, NARA M234, Roll 198.

40. Letter Lafayette Head to the CIA, December 8, 1865, NARA M234, Roll 198.

that agent Head, whom Cumming described as illiterate, may have originated the idea.[41]

In contrast to the attitude of later Colorado officials who wanted all Utes removed from their state, agent Head in 1864 recommended that the Muache, Capote and Wiminuche bands of Utes, then under the Indian Superintendency of New Mexico, be attached to the Tabeguache band at his Conejos agency. Head said that the Utes from New Mexico could occupy that portion of Colorado lying immediately south of the Elk Mountains, bounded on the east by the Saguache Mountains, and on the west by the Sierra San Miguel. Their territory would extend as far as the Uncompahgre Mountains, an area he said was interspersed with several mountains streams and valleys of sufficient fertility to be a good permanent home.[42] In the following years, Head again pressed the idea of bringing the Utes from New Mexico to Colorado.[43] A later Territorial Governor somehow got the idea that Washington in 1865 had approved the transfer to Colorado of at least the Muache band, and asked for a copy of the purported decision.[44] The misconception may have originated from the 1863 treaty provision by which the Tabeguache agreed to accept the Muache band onto their reservation.

Some idea of the operation of Head's agency in this period is provided by the estimate prepared by Agent Head of what he would require for the agency's operations in the fiscal year ending June 30, 1865: 50 head of beef cattle—$1,500; 300 head of sheep—$900; 200 fanagas of wheat—$600; pay for the agent—$1,500; hire of interpreter—$500; feeding of 4 publicly owned animals—$500; shoeing of 4 publicly owned animals—$25; office rent—$200; 15 cords of wood—$75; two boxes of candles—$30; stationary—$50. dollars. All this totaled $5,880. The foregoing figures are only for the operation of the agency, and do not cover any Government payments or gifts to the Tabeguache.[45] The annuities due the Tabeguache under Article 10 of the 1863 treaty were not being paid (the band had not moved to their reservation), but the government was still giving the Indians certain supplies. Head suggested that $5,000 be spent on goods for the Tabeguache as follows: $600 for rice, $240 for bread,

---

41. Letter Gov. Cumming to the CIA, February 21, 1866, NARA M234, Roll 198. Since Head later became the first elected Lieutenant Governor of Colorado, it seems doubtful that he was really illiterate.

42. Letter Head to the CIA, July 19, 1864, CIA, 1864, p. 240.

43. CIA, 1865, p. 13; Letter Head to Gov. Hunt, July 17,1867, CIA, 1867, p. 212.

44. Letter Gov. Hunt to the CIA, Jan. 24, 1868, NARA M234, Roll 199

45. Estimate dated July 22, 1863, NARA M234, Roll 197.

$500 for coffee, $1,500 for bacon sides, $600 for navy beans, $250 for dried apples, $500 for tea, $10 for unground black pepper, and $800 for sugar.[46]

Ouray at this time had not yet achieved predominant status among the Tabeguache. In correspondence in the summer of 1865, Governor Evans referred to the Indian known as Colorow as being head chief of the Tabeguache, or at least the head war chief.[47] When Evans' successor as Governor, Alexander Cumming, later in 1865 instructed agent Head to bring to Denver several prominent chiefs from Conejos for a conference, Cumming did not request Ouray by name.[48] The Utes whom Head subsequently brought to Denver early in 1866 to meet Cumming, were Shavano, described as the head war chief of the Tabeguache, and a young chief said to be the brother-in-law of Ouray.[49] No Ouray.

Besides thinking about bringing the New Mexico Utes into Colorado, Colorado officials also considered consolidating in one area those Utes already in Colorado. Cumming tried in the fall of 1866 to persuade the Utes served by the agency located at Middle Park to move in with the Tabeguache band. He ran into a firestorm. In a report to Washington on a council he held at the Middle Park with the White River and the Yampa Utes, Cumming wrote that those Utes "were exasperated to hear that the Tabeguache claimed to have the right to so many lands which they had sold to the government. They said that this great pretension was a great wrong and outrage upon them as a people. They said the Tabeguache had never sold the lands. If they had done so, they had no right whatsoever to do it. They said the country they were now occupying was their own hunting ground, that it was the only locality in which they could find game, and that no power should disturb them in their possession of it." Cumming said he persisted so long in the effort to induce these bands to leave their traditional lands and move to a reservation in the vicinity of the Tabeguache that he came to fear unpleasant consequences. So he settled for getting the Middle Park Utes to sign a treaty allowing roads to be made through their grounds, and agreeing not to disturb those engaged in such construction.[50]

Despite this failure, Cumming thought that getting the Colorado Utes together was a goal worth pursuing: "The only course to be pursued, in my opinion, is to unify all the different Ute bands into one body, and to offer such inducements as will ensure their concentration in the selected portion of the

---

46. Letter Head to Gov. Evans, August 15, 1865, NARA M234, Roll 198.
47. Letters Evans to the CIA, July 6 and July 9, 1865, NARA M234, Roll 198.
48. Letter Cumming to the CIA, Nov. 4, 1865, NARA M234, Roll 198.
49. Letter Cumming to the CIA, February 21, 1866, NARA M234, Roll 198.
50. Letter Cumming to the CIA, October 10, 1866 CIA, 1866, p. 154.

country. If the Tabeguache territory is not sufficient—and evidently it is not—then let it be enlarged or exchanged for another more spacious.... They cannot be allowed to remain as they are now on the borders of settlements, subject to all malign influences of bad men. In the second place, the demands of the people who are flocking into the country from every direction, along the foothills, the mountains, in the mines, and on the banks of every stream, require that they should be removed to prevent the constant uneasiness and occasional alarms that now prevail."[51] The next year, the Acting Commissioner of Indian Affairs endorsed such consolidation: "There should be no [need of] special legislation by Congress respecting the matter of colonizing all the tribes in Colorado in one locality; the efforts of the Department will be directed to the securing this at the earliest possible date."[52]

In 1866, Colorado Territory's sole delegate in the House of Representatives, A. A. Bradford, wrote to the Commissioner of Indian Affairs asking that he do something about the Utes served by the Middle Park Agency. Bradford said that significant mineral discoveries had been made there, and urged that the agency there be removed in order to clear the way for an overland mail line through the area.[53] A treaty with *all* the Utes again seemed necessary for clearing up the Indian situation in Colorado.

During 1866, Ouray began to set himself apart from Chief Shavano and to distinguish himself as a peacemaker. In June of that year, agent Head reported to Kit Carson, then Commandant at Fort Garland, that Shavano and his followers, not including Ouray, had committed depredations against Mexicans along the Huerfano River.[54] Later that autumn, Ouray took a leading role in keeping the peace when Muache chief Kaniache tried to enlist the Tabeguache for attacks on Mexican settlers in the San Luis Valley.[55] Ouray's actions have been variously

---

51. Letter Cumming to the CIA, October 10, 1866,CIA, 1866, p. 156.

52. CIA, 1867, p. 13

53. Letter Colorado Delegate Bradford to the CIA, June 15, 1866, NARA M234, Roll 198.

54. Letter Carson to the Aide de Camp in Santa Fe, June 14, 1866, Letters and Telegrams sent from Fort Garland, Volume 2 (hereafter simply Fort Garland), June 1866 to June 1869.

55. Virginia M. Simmons, *The Ute Indians of Utah, Colorado and New Mexico*, Boulder, University of Colorado Press, 2000, p. 125; Smith, *op. cit.*, p. 49; Thelma S. Guild and Harvey L. Carter, *Kit Carson, A Pattern for Heroes*, Lincoln, University of Nebraska Press, 1984, p. 272-3; Olive W. Burt, *Ouray, the Arrow*, New York, Julian Messner, Inc., 1953, p. 1.

described by various authors, but what Ouray actually did in this latter instance can most reliably be seen in the report that Carson sent to his military superiors in Santa Fe. Carson wrote that Ouray came to Fort Garland on October 6, 1866 and said he did not intend to join the fight started by Kaniache. Carson told Ouray to go back to his village, and bring all peaceful Indians to camp at Fort. Garland. Carson sent a sergeant to the village with Ouray to prevent any attack on him by Colonel Alexander, who was then closely pursuing Kaniache. On the ninth, Ouray returned with 100 lodges, and camped nine miles from Fort Garland. Ouray told Carson that he had sent a runner after Kaniache to tell him to quit fighting. Carson reported: "I sent a detachment out and ordered those Indians to camp near the post, which they did on the 10th. All peaceful Indians came in under the guidance of Ouray and they promised to return all the stock that had been taken…. Ouray was not only prompt in notifying me that he would keep the peace, but he also warned the settlers on the upper Huerfano to leave their ranches and put their stock in places of safety."

Ouray drew praise from another Army officer. In September, 1866 Quartermaster General James L. Rusling came to Colorado on an inspection trip for the Army. General Rusling met Ouray on September 21 at a small conference at Fort Garland which visiting General William Tecumseh Sherman had asked Fort Garland Commandant Carson to set up. Subsequently, Rusling went with Territorial Governor Cumming to a larger meeting with the Utes along the Rio Grande River, at which Cumming distributed the annual "presents." Some years later, Rusling published a book giving his very favorable impressions from these meetings with Ouray. Rusling wrote that the September 21 meeting at Fort Garland "lasted an hour or more, with much skillful fencing and adroit diplomacy on the part of Ouray and Ankatosh, the head chiefs.[56] About the later Rio Grande meeting, Rusling wrote: "The four leading men seemed to be Ouray (Arrow); Shawashawit (Blue Flower); Ankatosh, and Shavano. The head chief of the tribe, and the finest looking Indian I have seen, was Ouray. He was a medium-sized, athletic looking man of about 40 (note: Ouray was then about 33), with as fine an eye in the head as I have seen in anyone. Moreover, he was very neat and clean in his person, as if he believed in the saving virtues of soap and water. Two or three years before, he had made the tour of Washington and the east, and today wore the handsome silver medal that President Lincoln had given him. Kit Carson said that Ouray had made good use of this eastern trip, and was already a rising man. The knowledge acquired had since raised him to the kingship. Several chiefs were

---

56.   Ankatosh was actually a Muache, signing treaties as such.

older, but not so shrewd as he. The head warrior, however, was Ankatosh. He was one of the coolest and bravest looking men I ever met......Ouray certainly conducted himself with great dignity and good sense, for a untutored savage, and fully realized our old-time notions about an Indian Chief. Should he live, Ouray will yet make a figure among the Indians, and go down to history as a Logan or Red Jacket. His trip to Washington, he told me, convinced him that it was idle for his people to contend with the palefaces, and his counsel was always for peace and civilization. Subsequently, some months later, when the Utes rose in hostilities against his advice, he deliberately went to Fort Garland and gave himself up, refusing to have anything to do with the tribe until they laid down their arms again.[57]

Commandant's House, Fort Garland

Kit Carson kept in touch with Ouray whenever Indian questions arose. In 1867 when the officer in charge of the military district of New Mexico asked Carson about moving the Tabeguache out of the San Luis Valley as provided in the 1863 treaty, Carson replied that, through Ouray, he knew the Tabeguache were upset by the changes made by the Senate in the original text of the 1863 treaty. Carson warned Santa Fe that war should be expected if attempts were made to

57.   Rusling, *op. cit.*, p. 115.

move the Indians from the San Luis Valley. He added, however, that he would contact Ouray and get the latter to make a statement on any such move.[58]

A. Cameron Hunt, Cumming's successor as Territorial Governor, wrote to Washington in July, 1867 that the state of the Indians in Colorado was deplorable. Regarding the Tabeguache, Hunt said that the band was finding game very scarce. He complained that his messenger sent to Conejos reached that Agency only with great difficulty, having to swim across six streams, at risk to his life.[59] And Agent Head in July, 1867 reported to Governor Hunt that Fort Garland Commandant Carson had spoken of an outstanding order prohibiting any Ute Indians from roaming the eastern slope of the Rockies. Head did not criticize the order directly, but said it should not be enforced until the Tabeguache were moved across the Continental Divide to the reservation provided for in the 1863 Treaty.[60] Apparently, Carson was not enforcing the order.

Hunt wrote to Washington at the end of 1867, saying that as *ex officio* Superintendent of Indian Affairs in Colorado, he of course wanted to ensure that all supplies due the Colorado Indians from the federal government were delivered. But he complained that Washington had contracted the year before for the delivery of cattle from Texas to the Tabeguache. Yet as Governor of Colorado, he had to enforce a Colorado law banning the import of Texas cattle because of infectious fever, some outbreaks of which had already been seen in the southern part of the Territory.[61]

At the end of the year 1867, Governor Hunt came to Washington to prepare for a new negotiation with all the Utes, aimed at getting all seven recognized bands, from both Colorado and New Mexico, to agree to settle on one reservation in Colorado. The hope was that a selected delegation of Ute chiefs and head men, brought to Washington, would accept language surrendering most of Ute land in Colorado. The Ute delegates hopefully would sign the text in Washington, and then go home to sell it to their fellow tribesmen. No freewheeling negotiations with large bands of Utes at some remote site, as Governor Evans had done at Conejos in 1863.

In December, 1867, from Washington, Gov. Hunt asked Indian Commissioner Taylor for $2,000 to defray the expenses of assembling and transporting to Washington representatives of the seven Ute bands for "consultation, and per-

58. Letter Carson to James H. Carleton, commanding the district of New Mexico, February 15, 1867, Fort Garland, p. 84.
59. Letter Hunt to the CIA, July 4, 1867, NARA M234, Roll 199.
60. Letter Head to Hunt, July 17,1867, CIA, 1867, p. 212.
61. Letter Hunt to the CIA, December 17, 1867, NARA M234, Roll 199.

haps for a treaty."[62] Subsequently, Hunt asked the Commissioner Indian of Affairs to furnish six satchels and 10 pairs of gloves for the use of the Ute delegation in Washington.[63] Hunt obliquely hinted that the Ute chiefs would like to meet the President, and asked that "a four horse vehicle of some kind be engaged, for one or more days, to carry the Indians and attendants around the city so that the magnitude of the American capital may be more fully understood by them, and related by them to their various bands on their return to the mountains."[64] Hunt also proposed that the Indians and their attendants go home by way of New York, Boston and Niagara Falls, with stops at each place, "to give them a correct idea of the magnitude of United States and the wealth and power of our people. I also desire to show them the Springfield, Massachusetts armory and the manner and facilities we possess of manufacturing arms and munitions of war. A present of one first-class muzzle loading rifle and accouterments to each member the delegation would be the most fitting reward for their good behavior."[65] This same idea of showing the Ute delegation U.S. military power was also behind Hunt's request that the Secretary of the Interior ask the Secretaries of War and Navy to approve delegation visits to the Armory and the Navy Yard in Washington.[66]

Although Governor Hunt had criticized Ouray's linguistic abilities, saying that Ouray spoke very little English and not much more Spanish[67] he did include Ouray among those to be brought to Washington. Hunt probably underestimated Ouray's linguistic ability, as in later years, Ouray seems to have picked up considerable English, and did learn to sign his name. Hunt may not have thought Ouray a good interpreter, but seemed to consider him a leader.

The railroad in 1868 extended much further west than the terminus at St. Joseph, Missouri used by the Ute delegation in 1863. But Denver itself still had no rail connections. Leaving Denver, the new Ute delegation went by stagecoach to Cheyenne, where they caught a Union Pacific train for the East.[68] Hunt's preparations were rewarded when the treaty was signed in Washington on March

---

62.   Letter Hunt to the CIA, December 10, 1867, NARA M234, Roll 199.
63.   *Ibid.*.
64.   Letter Hunt to the CIA, Feb. 4, 1868, NARA M234, Roll 199.
65.   *Ibid.*
66.   Letter Secretary of the Interior to the CIA, February 6, 1868, NARA M234, Roll 199.
67.   Letter Hunt to the CIA, September 30, 1868, NARA M234, Roll 200.
68.   Olive Burt, *Ouray, the Arrow,* Julian Messner, Inc., New York, N. Y., 1953, p. 67-68.

2, 1868.[69] Among the signers for the United States, besides Governor Hunt, were Kit Carson, Commandant at Fort Garland, Head, and the agent from the other Colorado agency at Middle Park. Signing (by mark) for the Utes were 10 chiefs and headmen brought to Washington, representing all seven Ute bands. This time the first Indian to put his X mark on the document was Ouray. This does not necessarily mean that Ouray was "head chief of the Ute Nation," perhaps only that Ouray felt more at ease in Washington than his peers, and/or more convinced that signing was the right thing to do.

The most important provisions of the 1868 treaty were these. In Article 2, the United States agreed that, if the Utes gave up in Article 3, any claim to land elsewhere in Colorado, the United States would "set apart for the absolute and undisturbed use of the Utes, and for such other friendly tribes or individual Indians that they, with U.S. consent, may admit among them," the southwestern part of Colorado Territory, totaling about 25 percent of all the land in the Territory. Article 2 set the eastern boundary of the reservation at the 107th meridian west of Greenwich. On the west, the reservation would reach the Colorado-Utah boundary. The southern reservation boundary was specified as the 38th parallel of north latitude (the Colorado-New Mexico boundary). The northern reservation limit would run along an unmarked east-west line 15 miles north of the 40th parallel of north latitude, thus well short of the Colorado-Wyoming border. The Indian chiefs who signed this treaty probably understood only vaguely what parallels of latitude and meridians of longitude were. They would have been more comfortable with boundaries specified, as in the 1863 treaty, in terms of prominent geographic features. Even those who signed the new treaty for the U. S. Government did not know precisely where the specified reservation boundaries would run, an invitation for later troubles as we shall see.

The 1868 reservation for all the Utes was larger than that given the Tabeguache under the 1863 Treaty, as amended. The 1868 reservation extended well north of the Colorado River, which had been the northern boundary of the 1863 Tabeguache reservation, and also further west than the Gunnison-Uncompahgre River line, the western boundary of that 1863 reservation. These extensions presumably were to satisfy the Yampa, Grand River and Uintah bands. The southern boundary of the 1868 reservation was the New Mexico line, well south of where the 1863 Tabeguache reservation had ended along the ridge separating the drainage of the Rio Grande and Uncompahgre Rivers from the San Juan River. This

---

69.   15 Stat.619.

southerly extension presumably was to accommodate the interests of the Muache, Capote and Wiminuche bands.

In Article 4, the United States undertook to maintain two agencies[70] in Colorado to serve the various Ute bands. One agency, the White River agency, would serve the Yampa, Uintah and Grand River bands of Utes, collectively thereafter called the White River Utes. The other agency, to be on the Rio de Los Pinos, was to serve the other four recognized Ute bands, the Tabeguache, Muache, Capote and Wiminuche. Articles 10, 11 and 12 of the agreement laid out the compensation the Government would pay the Utes. This was to some extent time limited, and initially amounted to $60,000 per year. For the Tabeguache, Articles 1 and 17 were of particular importance. Article 1 said the 1863 treaty with the Tabeguache remained in force, to the extent it was not inconsistent with the 1868 treaty. Article 17 contained a hooker: the benefits due the Tabeguache under the 1863 treaty were now apportioned among all seven Ute bands.

The 1868 treaty was ratified in the Senate on July 25, 1868, but with one amendment. This withdrew certain lands that the U.S. had agreed to give the Indians during the March negotiations. This change meant that Governor Hunt had to revisit all the Indians to get their consent to the Senate change. A lot of travel for him, but no great difficulty in collecting the signatures. On November 6, 1868, President Andrew Johnson proclaimed the treaty in force.

On the very day the treaty was signed, Governor Hunt began an effort to get the government to give the Tabeguache some of the things promised them in the 1863 treaty, as amended.[71] Hunt specifically asked that $45,000 be made available to carry out the government promises to provide stock to the Tabeguache. The Commissioner of Indian Affairs endorsed Hunt's idea and forwarded the recommendation to the Secretary of Interior.[72] The latter rejected the idea, saying that until the Tabeguache were on the 1863 reservation and engaged in agriculture, they had no claim to the benefits provided in Article 10 of the 1863 treaty.[73]

So on his return to Denver, Hunt had three Tabeguache chiefs (Ouray was one), and three Muache chiefs (Kaniache was one) sign a statement saying that for four years, their people had been willing to move "to their new home on the Uncompahgre River," and were still ready to do so, if they were given what had

---

70. This was no additional burden on the government; two agencies had been in operation before.
71. Letter Hunt to the CIA, Washington D.C., March 2, 1868, NARA M234, Roll 199.
72. Letter CIA to the Secretary of Interior, March 17, 1868, NARA M234, Roll 199.
73. Letter Secretary of Interior to the CIA, March 24, 1868, NARA M234, Roll 199.

been promised them, and if their agent were instructed to go with them.[74] Note: although the Muache were not parties to the 1863 treaty, the authorities had long hoped the Muache and Tabeguache would settle together. This action seemed to show that Hunt did not view a signature by Ouray alone as sufficient to commit even the Tabeguache, so he brought in two other Tabeguache chiefs, the well known Guero and a far less known third. Finally, the statement envisioned that the new agency for the Tabeguache and others would be located in the Uncompahgre Valley, not on the Rio de los Pinos as specified in the 1868 Treaty.

The signing of this treaty again brought the question to the fore: how could all the Utes be moved to the new reservation? Moving the Tabeguache took priority; they seemed to be the most ready to settle down, and their agency at Conejos was located in a more heavily populated area of Colorado. Lafayette Head resigned as agent to the Tabeguache after the signing of the 1868 treaty, as he did not want to move away from Conejos because of his long established business there. So Governor Hunt perforce became more directly involved with the band. In July, 1868 he moved the Tabeguache agency from Conejos to the Saguache valley, saying the move was made at the request of Ouray.[75] Of course, the move helped Hunt, as Saguache was closer to Hunt's home base in Denver than Conejos had been.

Hunt met with the Tabeguache on the Saguache River on July 12 and 13, 1868. He reported to Washington that he received assurances that the Tabeguache were not only willing, but anxious to go the reservation and remain permanently. They only wanted assurance that their agent would go with them, and show that he had the means to prevent them from perishing from cold and hunger during the five months of each year when the band would be shut off from all sources of supply. Hunt urged that $3,000 be set aside for constructing agency buildings on the Uncompahgre River, a site within the new reservation, and that the agent to the Tabeguache with his employees be required to reside there permanently.[76] Hunt also pointed out that the agency locations specified in the treaty were remote, and difficult to supply with goods.[77]

---

74. Formal statement by 3 Chiefs of the Tabeguache and 3 Chiefs of the Muache, signed in the presence of Governor Hunt, Daniel Oakes, Lafayette Head, C. Case, with U. M. Curtis, special interpreter present, April 4, 1868, NARA M234, Roll 199.
75. Letter Hunt to the CIA, July 25, 1868, Annual Report of the CIA, 1869, p. 182.
76. Letter Hunt to the CIA, July 25, 1868, CIA,1868, p. 182.
77. Letter Hunt to the CIA, April 9, 1869, NARA M234, Roll 200.

2

The Los Pinos Agency Established, at the Wrong Place

Alexander Hunt was replaced as Colorado Territorial Governor and Superintendent of Indian Affairs by Edward M. McCook in April, 1869, not long after Ulysses S. Grant took office as President. McCook would not hold his Superintendent title long, as this office was abolished in 1870.[1] A Territorial Governor who was also Superintendent of Indian Affairs faced a conflict of interest in having to chose between protecting the rights of his Indian charges, who could not vote, and the often opposing desires of settlers, who did vote.

Governor McCook in June, 1869 informed the Office of Indian Affairs of his plans for establishing the Tabeguache agency at a new site believed to be within the set reservation boundaries. He envisaged an agency surrounded by a stockade to protect agency employees against hostile Cheyenne or Arapahos. He said that he thought adobe would be best construction material for the reservation buildings, since adobe did not burn.[2] Making plans for the new agency was one thing, getting the Utes to go there was something else. McCook, at the request of the chiefs, met a number of Utes, some 2,000 of whom camped for some days near Denver in July, 1869. McCook reported to Washington that "I held two councils within them in which, although they expressed great satisfaction at the number of goods given them, they said they did not desire to go the reservation. They thought they would be too far from Denver if the agencies are located at the points designated in the treaties. During the first council I had, two of the chiefs expressed their dissatisfaction at the replacement of agent Head. Ouray, the head chief of the Tabeguache and the most intelligent and influential man of the whole Ute nation, took a softer line. Ouray said that although his band would keep their promise and go to reservation, the Capotes had never received any

---

1. Hill, *op. cit.*, p. 47.
2. Letter McCook to the CIA, June 20,1869, NARA M234, Roll 199.

annuities from the whites and denied having signed any treaties. He thought there would be great difficulty in getting the Capotes onto the reservation."[3] Note here that Ouray was looking beyond parochial Tabeguache matters.

In June, 1869, Army Lt. Calvin T. Speer was named to replace the long-serving agent Lafayette Head. It fell to Speer in July to try to persuade the Utes to move, finally, to the western side of the Continental Divide and onto their new reservation. Speer met them at the Saguache River, and reported that initially, the Utes did not want him, a white man, to go onto their reservation. They also objected to his building an agency on their reservation, saying that no whites were to be allowed there. On the first day, Speer said he had to spend some six hours in council before he could get Ouray, who usually took the lead in such talks, to make any reply whatsoever. At last, Ouray said that the whole party had better remain at the Saguache, as it would not be safe to precede further. Speer reported that the Capotes, the Muache and the Wiminuche were especially stubborn and ill natured, saying that they could take care themselves and did not ask the government for one cent worth of aid. They said that they had often been deceived and robbed by the representatives of the government. Major Head had plundered them, Governor Cumming had taken part, and Governor Hunt had taken everything. They alleged that now also Lt. Speer was deceiving them to get them to go to the reservation.[4] Was there any truth to this Ute charge about Cumming? The House Interior Committee later held a hearing into allegations that Cumming was involved in financial irregularities involving Indians in Colorado. However, Cumming was charged with fraud against the Government, not against the Utes.[5]

Finally, Speer persuaded at least the Tabeguache to move up to the headwaters of Saguache River, across the Cochetopa Pass to a stream rising on the northeast slope of the San Juan Mountains. Lt. Speer reported that from the new agency

---

3.   Letter McCook to the CIA, July 28, 1869, NARA M234, Roll 199.

4.   Letter McCook to the CIA, Aug. 25, 1869, NARA M234, Roll 200.

5.   The House Indian Affairs Committee held hearings in February, 1867, on charges made by Colorado delegate Bradford. The charges did not involve any action Cumming took in respect to the Indians, but basically that he misused Government funds. Allegedly, Cumming approved payment of excessive bills for such things as freight and office rent, and used Government money to hire his daughter and 14-year old son to work on Indian matters. Ex-Governors Gilpin and Evans, and future Governor Hunt were called to testify. The report of the Committee in March, 1867, ended inconclusively with a long exculpatory letter from Cumming. House Miscellaneous Document 81, 39th Congress, 2nd Session, tabled March 2, 1867.

site "a beautiful valley stretched 40 to 50 miles north westward, with much good agricultural land. A saw mill was being built there to prepare lumber for a new agency, with the agency buildings expected to be finished by the end of October.[6] All objections of the Indians to going onto the reservation have ceased, and 120 lodges now dot the mountain side. All expressed a degree of satisfaction at the idea of having a home that is really surprising. I furnished them, as you directed, some bread and beef, and suggest that a sufficient supply of bread, beef, potatoes and beans be constantly kept for them."[7]

Following up in October, Governor McCook told Washington that good progress had been made in establishing the new agency at its selected site. He wrote that the saw mill at the site was completed, along with a warehouse. Also the other buildings were about ready. He said that when all were finished, the saw mill would be used to make lumber to be sold to whites in exchange for food for the Indians.[8] McCook decided to fire all the civilian employees who had worked at the Tabeguache Agency at Conejos and Saguache, telling Washington that he thought they had all engaged in dishonest and deceptive practices under the former administration.[9]

Although McCook had approvingly quoted Lt. Speer's report of finding a good site for the new agency called for in the 1868 treaty, he came to dislike this location because of the difficulty of access, something Governor Hunt had pointed out earlier. Wagons trains carrying the supplies to the Los Pinos agency took 10 to 11 days from the town of Saguache. The location was poor for other reasons.

---

6.   Letter McCook to the CIA, July 28, 1869 quoting Speer's report to him, NARA M234, roll 200.
7.   Letter Speer to McCook, Sept. 1, 1869, 1870, Report of the CIA, p. 265.
8.   Letter McCook to the CIA, October 16, 1869, NARA M234, roll 200.
9.   Letter McCook to the CIA, Oct. 16, 1869, CIA, 1869, pp. 267 to 269.

Site of Los Pinos Agency, 1869-75

Lt. Speer claimed that the new agency site had good agricultural land as well as much timber. Later experience showed the site selected was a bad choice, if the Indians were expected to take up agriculture. The Commandant at Fort Garland charged that the site had been selected to suit speculators and contractors, and that it was too bleak for even Indians to live there.[10] The Fort Garland Commandant was not alone in being unhappy about the Cochetopa tributary site for the new agency, which came to be called the Los Pinos Agency although nowhere near the real Rio de los Pinos. In 1870, the legislative assembly of New Mexico Territory petitioned the U.S. Senate and House to relocate the Agency to the vicinity of the San Juan River, and remonstrated against its location elsewhere. The petition argued that "The most powerful and important bands of the Utah nation are those of the Capotes and the Wiminuche, who allege that they never consented to said treaty, and declared that it is fraudulent and without effect. The buildings intended for the agency and the mills have already been erected at great cost to the government upon a small tributary of the River Cochetopa, at a distance of at least 100 leagues from the Rio de Los Pinos, upon which, according to

---

10.   Letter Commanding Officer at Fort Garland to the Assistant Adjutant General, District of New Mexico, Sept. 4,1872, NARA M234. Roll 202.

the stipulation to the treaty, the agency was to be situated. Furthermore the sheep and cows have not been furnished for the Indians. In view of this, the Utah positively refused to settle upon the reservation placed as it is, and demand that the same be located on the Rio de Los Pinos, as is positively specified in the treaty and which is in the midst of their ancient hunting grounds. They declare they will oppose, with arms in their hands, any proceeding whatever that is made to compel them to settle on the reservation on the River Cochetopa."[11] Nevertheless, the so-called Los Pinos agency remained on the feeder of the Cochetopa for several more years, while many Utes continued to roam about in New Mexico Territory, avoiding the Los Pinos Agency supposed to serve them. Naming the Cochetopa feeder creek "Los Pinos" was not enough to draw the New Mexico Utes.

McCook and Speer did get the agency buildings erected on Los Pinos creek, which they thought was within the boundaries of reservation specified in the 1868 treaty. Governor McCook had this to say about the location of the new agency: "The agency is about 165 miles northwest from Fort Garland by the only traveled road (through Saguache Village).There is no difficulty in transporting goods as far as Saguache, but the road from there to the agency is one of the worst I ever saw. Crossing Cochetopa Pass, the pass Fremont crossed with his party in 1842, and following the old Salt Lake trail some 35 or 40 miles, then turning south or a little west of south…looking at the map of Utah and Colorado, prepared by order of General Sherman in 1869, you find the location of the agency; it is on the third stream west of the 107th meridian, laid down on the map as a tributary of the Grand River. The explorers and guides of the country stated to me, however, that the map was wrong, and that the Grand River is much further north."[12] Governor McCook was under the impression that the new agency was west of the 107th meridian and thus within the prescribed boundaries of the new reservation. Either McCook did not know where the agency actually sat, or else the Sherman map was wrong in more than one way. When 4 years later, the General Land Office hired a surveyor to mark out the Reservation boundary at the 107th meridian, the agency was indeed found to be east, not west, of that meridian and hence outside the specified reservation boundaries. But there were other, more obvious defects with the chosen site, principally that its altitude was too high to encourage the Indians to settle around it and engage in agriculture. Speer

---

11. Senate Miscellaneous Document 97, (41-2), serial set 1408.
12. Letter McCook to the CIA, Oct. 16, 1869, Annual Report of the CIA, pages 267 to 269.

did not attempt to spend the winter at the new agency. Located at about 9,000 feet, winter came early there and lingered long. His term as agent would be short.

President Ulysses S. Grant in 1869 adopted a more relaxed Indian policy, and established the Board of Indian Commissioners by Executive Order, with the approval of the Congress. Religious denominations would have influence over appointments to this Board. Grant also decided that Army officers would no longer be detailed as Indian agents, and that Protestant religious denominations would be asked to nominate candidates for agents. This practice would no doubt be challenged today on Constitutional grounds, but it was accepted then. The Unitarian Church in Boston was asked to propose candidates for the two Colorado agencies.

The Unitarian headquarters in Boston chose one of its ministers, Jabez Nelson Trask, for the Tabeguache Agency,[13] still located at the spot chosen by Lt. Speer in 1869. Trask had been born October 19, 1831 in Freedom, Maine. He attended the Phillips Exeter Academy, and entered Harvard College in 1859 as a sophomore. He graduated with a bachelor's degree in 1862. During the summers of 1863 and 1864, he worked as a civil servant at Port Royal, South Carolina, with the mission of protecting abandoned property as well as seeing that former slaves left to fend for themselves were fed and educated.[14] Trask subsequently attended the Harvard Divinity School, receiving a degree in 1866. His initial career in the ministry was short; he spent 1868-69 at the Unitarian church at New Salem, Massachusetts, and then four months at the Unitarian church in West Cummington, Massachusetts.[15] Trask did not like his first name, and signed his name either as J. Nelson Trask or simply as J. N. Trask. The latter is how he was recorded in the 1870 census, which listed him as 39 years old, single, by occupation a minister, and living in the home of a druggist in Ward 4 in St. Joseph, Missouri.[16] Trask was still in St. Joseph in the spring of 1871 when he was appointed Agent at Los Pinos.

Trask showed up at the Indian Affairs office in Lawrence, Kansas, in April, 1871, without funds and asking for money to pay his way to Colorado.[17] He wangled free railroad tickets to Denver, and then walked on foot most of the way

13. Letter American Unitarian Association to the CIA, March 17, 1871, M234, Roll 201.

14. Handwritten Trask letter, February 24, 1908 in the Harvard University Archives.

15. Fiftieth Anniversary Report of the Harvard Class of 1862, 1912, Cambridge, MA.

16. 1870 Census, Roll 762, page 602, line 23.

17. Telegram Superintendent of Indian Affairs for Kansas to the CIA, April 6, 1871, NARA M234, Roll 201.

from Denver to his agency. There he showed traits which made some think him mad. He reportedly had "enormous green goggles and buckthorn stick...he walked around, glowering at everybody, in a navy blue swallow tail coat with brass buttons...and an ancient, broad-brimmed Puritan hat."[18] After Colorado Governor McCook lost his position as Superintendent of Indian Affairs, Trask dared to criticize the Governor in letters to Washington. Risky. Even though McCook was no longer his direct boss, he was still a person with political clout that a wiser man than Trask would not have antagonized. In one letter referring to a recent speech by McCook, Trask not only charged that McCook was anti-Ute, but commented that "the English language will live through the Governor's maltreatment of it."[19] Trask somehow got the idea that his mail was being tampered with, and developed a feud with the nearest Post Office, that at Saguache. He wrote Washington that he would travel the extra 85 miles to Fort Garland if he had something important to mail.[20]

But Trask was not without a good side. He called attention to many deficiencies at the Los Pinos Agency arising before his arrival. He termed keeping stock at the Agency in large herds, unsheltered and unfed, a cruelty and a hazard. He said that while several winters might pass without one of the animals dying from cold or starvation, the young stock suffered every winter; a severe winter will decimate them. Coyotes and gray wolves take some of the best from the herders. "Agriculture here cannot be at all depended on for subsistence. I think the agency is at perhaps 8,000 (actually 9,000) feet above sea level. Between grasshoppers in May and June, and frost in August, I have only succeeded in raising potatoes, of which a common spoon will hold six at a time. Grasshoppers have been very numerous during the last three seasons." He called the saw mill, said by his predecessor to be in prime order, unserviceable. "The building had to be braced against the wind lest it blow down." The roof of the warehouse he said was partially collapsed. All the buildings, although only 2 years old, he called decrepit.[21]

Unlike Speer, Trask stayed at the agency over winter, even though no Indians came there. In the winter of 1871-72, Trask noted that the last Indian went away

18.   Marshall Sprague, *Massacre: the Tragedy at White River*, Little, Brown and Co., Boston, 1957, p. 106, as quoted by Robert H. Keller, Jr., *American Protestantism and United States Indian Policy, 1869-82*, University of Nebraska Press, Lincoln, 1983, p. 65.
19.   Letter Trask to the CIA, Feb. 13, 1872, NARA M234, Roll 202.
20.   Letter Trask to the CIA, April 25, 1872, NARA M234, Roll 202.
21.   Letter Trask to the Chief Clerk of the Office of Indian Affairs, Sept. 11, 1871, CIA, 1871, pp. 554-555.

in November, and none returned to the site until mid-April. He wrote of skiing (or as he put it, using "snow skates") the 25 miles or so between the agency and the cattle camp on the Gunnison River, at a much lower altitude. When near winter's end, he visited the herder at the cattle camp, Trask was the first living person the herder had seen in 66 days.[22] At Los Pinos, Trask at least had the handful of employees of the agency to socialize with, if he wanted to.

Trask's submission for the Annual Report of the Commissioner of Indian Affairs in 1871 suggests problems in relating to his Indian charges. Trask proudly noted that he did "not drink whiskey, smoke or chew tobacco, though I always given a half of my house to the Indians for smoking and sleeping, forbidding smoking only my office. I have designedly made no special presents to the Indians for the purchase of good will....They ceased to ask for presents long ago. I hope that this would wean them from the disposition to beg and be hangers-on." He said he had not seen any opportunity for missionary work among the Indians, but had gotten them to respect Sunday as a day of rest. He said the Indians were not interested in work or school. He noted that there is much work to be done, but nobody to do it, the men not being active.[23] Other than getting the Indians to take Sunday off, Trask's reports do not show much accomplishment.

Washington became worried about problems at Trask's agency, while conceding that some were perhaps due to failings of Trask's predecessor, Lt. Speer. Whatever, the Secretary of the Interior decided that the Office of Indian Affairs should send someone to help Trask straighten things out.[24] The inspector sent to investigate reported that, shortly before he reached the agency site, some Indians came out to meet him to complain about Trask. In a conversation the inspector had with Chief Ouray, the latter asked that Trask "be sent home to his friends," and that Col. Pfeiffer, a former agent in New Mexico, be appointed in his place. In the end, the inspector decided that Trask was not mad, but conceded he was eccentric.[25]

Trask may have been a minister in the Unitarian Church, but he proved himself capable of enduring the difficult living conditions at the Los Pinos Agency. He did not complain about his house being drafty, or having to sit on boxes, as his successor would do later. Trask had some good ideas. Trask said the agency was poorly situated for agriculture, although fine for lumbering. At a time when his agency was called by Colorado officials simply "the Lower Ute Agency,"[26] he

---

22. Letter Trask to the CIA, April 10, 1872, NARA M234, Roll 202.
23. *ibid.*
24. Letter Secretary of Interior to the CIA, July 29, 1871, NARA M234, Roll 201.
25. Letter Inspector to the CIA, Sept. 30, 1871, NARA M234, Roll 201.
26. Letter Gov. McCook to the CIA, Oct. 16, 1871, NARA M234, Roll 202.

suggested that it be renamed "Cochetope," after the name of the closest pass, creek, and mountains. He urged that, as the first step to permanent settlement of the Tabeguache, the exact location of the 107th meridian be determined, which by the 1868 treaty was the eastern boundary of the reservation. Trask said that nobody there knew within at least 20 miles where the meridian ran. He pointed out that the Indians still considered the mountain range west of the San Luis valley, the Cochetopas, as the true boundary, and understood nothing of meridians.[27]

The Indians kept complaining about Agent Trask, and Chief Ouray even wrote to President Grant to urge that he be replaced.[28] The Commissioner of Indian Affairs wrote the Secretary of Interior in January, 1872 urging that steps be taken to replace Trask.[29] Trask understood that Ouray did not like him and was pleased to report to Washington in May, 1872 that, on returning to the agency from one of his periodic trips to Saguache, he encountered Ouray. Trask proudly noted that he and Ouray rode together for a distance, and that Ouray invited him into his tent that evening.[30]

The position of Indian Agent was one requiring nomination by the President and confirmation by the Senate, so the Commissioner of Indian Affairs could not, on his own, remove an unsatisfactory agent. The Secretary of Interior the wrote the Unitarian Association in Boston to ask that they name a replacement for Trask.[31] The Unitarians were reluctant to move against Trask, and in April, 1872, asked their Member of Congress to look into the charges against Trask.[32] Finally, the Unitarians agreed "respectfully" to recommend Governor McCook's candidate, one Charles Adams, as Trask's replacement.[33] It is not clear that the Unitarian Association knew anything about Adams. Adams was not a Unitarian although he had previously served as acting agent to the Middle Park Utes.

---

27. Letter Trask to the CIA, May 13, 1871, NARA M234, Roll 201.
28. Letter Ouray to President Grant, June 19, 1871, NARA Microfilm Publication M808, Interior Records on Appointments in Colorado, Roll 13. Hereinafter NARA M808.
29. Letter Walker to the Secretary of Interior, January 15, 1872, NARA M808, Roll 13.
30. Letter Trask to the CIA, May 8, 1872, NARA M234, Roll 202.
31. Letter Fox, Acting Secretary of Unitarian Association, to the Secretary of Interior, January 18, 1872, NARA M808, Roll 13.
32. Letter Shippen, Secretary of the Unitarian Association, to the Acting CIA, April 22, 1872, NARA M808, Roll 13.
33. Telegram Shippen, Secretary of the Unitarian Association, to the Indian Bureau, Department of Interior May 16, 1872, NARA M808, Roll 13.

While the Trask controversy was going on, moves were afoot in Washington to get more land away from the Utes. Prospectors were coming into the Ute reservation, finding presumably valuable mineral deposits. On February 19, 1872, Colorado Delegate Chaffee proposed a bill,[34] which passed in April, providing for negotiations with the Utes.[35] The idea was to get the Utes to cede a chunk of their reservation encompassing the San Juan Mountains where many mineral discoveries were being made. Pursuant to this Act, Washington in June appointed three men as members of a commission to persuade the Utes to "cede" this strip. The commission was headed by Territorial Governor Edward McCook. Originally, the idea was to have a negotiating council with all the Utes at Pagosa Springs in mid-August,[36] but this site was abandoned in July in favor of the Los Pinos agency.[37] When the negotiators reached Fort Garland on August 20, 1872, McCook wrote to Los Pinos agent Adams to be sure that the supplies had arrived which had been ordered for the Indians to help the negotiations along (the goods had not arrived).

McCook and his group, to which Lafayette Head and other local citizens considered to have the trust of the Utes had been added, met with most of the bands of Utes at the Los Pinos agency at the end of August. The Wiminuche did not show up, supposedly hiding in Utah following the murder of an Indian agent at the Navajo agency in Arizona.[38] During the negotiations, McCook and his group ran into firm opposition from the assembled Utes. In his report to Washington, McCook said that Article 16 of the 1868 treaty requiring that any new surrender of Ute land be ratified by at least 3/4 of all Ute males was a major obstacle. He said this might be overcome by sending men of influence to meet separately with the various Ute bands.[39] In his report, the Commandant at Fort Garland, who also attended, did not speak highly of the commission. He wrote that they had left the Indians irritated, although they did manage to extract a promise from the Indians that the trespassing miners would not be molested. The Commandant also noted that intruding miners were not the only problem; an Englishman had taken a herd of 3,000 cattle into one of the parks on the Ute reservation.[40]

---

34. HR 102, 42nd Congress, 2nd session.

35. 15 Stat. 55.

36. Telegram McCook to the CIA, July 20,1872, NARA M234, Roll 202.

37. Letter W. F. C. Arny to the CIA, July 27,1872, NARA M234, Roll 202.

38. Letter W. C. F. Arny to the Commissioners appointed to negotiate with the Utes, Aug. 28,1872, NARA M234, Roll 202.

39. CIA, 1872, pp. 123-124.

40. Letter Commanding Officer at Fort Garland to the Assistant Adjutant General, District of New Mexico, Sept. 17,1872, NARA M234, Roll 202.

The year 1872 was marked by failures, of Agent Trask in his relations with the Tabeguache, and of Governor McCook in his attempt to get the Utes to cede the mining areas of the San Juan Mountains. Trask's shortcomings apparently were not typical of agents nominated by religious denominations. By 1873, when some 65 persons nominated by religious groups had become agents, the Commissioner of Indian Affairs wrote that those making the nominations were aware of their serious obligations towards the government, and that if a bad apple turned up, the nominating church was usually the first to suggest replacement.[41]

The appointment of Trask's successor, Charles Adams, was dated May 28, 1872. Trask left Los Pinos in the summer of 1872. He was subsequently ordained by the Unitarians and given a ministerial appointment at New Salem, Massachusetts. He married Lydia Maria Stratton there in 1873. When Lydia died in 1900, Trask moved to Orange, Massachusetts. In his later life, he did a variety of things, from being a volunteer weather observer to surveying for construction of sewers in Dorchester, Massachusetts. He often startled his fellows during town meetings by taking views radically different from the majority. He was wont to criticize town officers in the local paper.[42] Trask died in Massachusetts General Hospital in Boston at age 76. Trask willed his body to the Harvard Medical School, and his estate to the Society for the Protection of Animals.[43]

As Trask had done, so Charles Adams did not have kind words to say about his predecessor. Adams blamed Trask for not using his influence to calm the Indians down when they feared being driven from the reservation by the influx of miners seeking silver and gold. Adams wrote that "if their former agent, instead of trying to allay the fears of the whites by writing recriminating articles to the press, had used his authority to quiet the fears of the Indians, all this trouble could have been avoided, and the territory of Colorado enriched with some hundreds or thousands of immigrants…. The saw mill, formerly reported as unserviceable, now is running full capacity, cutting 2,500 feet per day."[44]

Adams' contribution to the 1873 report of the Commissioner of Indian Affairs reported much progress in relations between agent and Indians. Adams said he had set up a school in 1872, and reported that on some days, as many as 20 of the enrolled 40 children showed up. Some students were even there as boarders, and these students had made good progress in learning English. He said that attendance had fallen off when a smallpox epidemic forced him to move the

---

41.   CIA, 1873, p. 9.
42.   50th Anniversary Report, Class of 1862, Harvard University, Cambridge, 1912.
43.   Newspaper report, March 18, 1909 from Harvard University Archives.
44.   Letter Adams to the CIA, Sept. 6, 1872, CIA, 1872, pp 289 to 291.

school some miles way from the agency site. He also noted that the cattle herd, numbering 509 head when received from Trask, now numbered 741. He praised Ouray for ordering the Indians not to attack trespassers on the reservation, and for hospitably receiving at the agency parties of surveyors, miners, explorers, and military groups. He reported that by counting all fresh arrivals during the summer, he determined that the following numbers of Utes of the various bands visited Los Pinos for the purpose of obtaining supplies: Tabeguache: 423 men, 557 women, 1,024 children; Muache: 78 men, 113 women, 256 children; Capotes: 26 men, 31 women, 72 children; and Wiminuche: 23 men, 19 women, 41 children. The total for the three bands: 550 men, 720 women, 1,393 children.[45] So some New Mexico Utes did come the Los Pinos agency, despite vows not to do so unless the agency moved to the true Rio de los Pinos.

Like Trask, Adams saw no possibility of successful agriculture in the vicinity of the Agency, because of the altitude. He noted that along the Uncompahgre, Delores, and La Plata streams, all well within the Reservation, good crops had been raised by the few Indians living there. But he also said that the abundance of game still attracts the majority of the Utes, that only necessity would force the majority to become tillers of the soil.[46]

Adams showed his regard for Chief Ouray in May, 1873. He recommended that Washington compensate Ouray for losses suffered when a log house Ouray was temporarily occupying at the agency burned down. Adams said that the probable cause of the fire was a defective spot in the chimney. Adams recommended that, in view of the great services rendered by Ouray, this loss should be made good to him out of funds for beneficial purposes, as Ouray was at the agency on official duty at the time.[47]

Charles Adams was a friend of Governor McCook (indeed, his brother-in-law) and had witnessed at first hand McCook's failure at his agency in August, 1872 to secure Ute cession of the San Juan Mountain region. Adams wanted to reverse this setback. Prospectors were flooding into the San Juans, and Adams wanted Washington to do something about the intruders. In March, 1873, Adams suggested that the principal Ute chiefs be invited to Washington for new negotiations on giving up the San Juan area, an idea he had advanced as early as September, 1872.[48] In a report to Washington in April, 1873, Adams praised Washington's reaction to his concern about trespassing miners: "I feel very grati-

45.   Letter Adams to the CIA, Sept. 26, 1873,CIA, 1873, pp. 257-260.
46.   *Ibid.*
47.   Letter Adams to the CIA, May 18, 1873, NARA M234, Roll 203.
48.   Letter Adams to McCook, Sept. 10,1872, NARA M234, Roll 202.

fied in regard to the action taken by the government concerning the San Juan mining district, and I think this very order will have more effect on them (i.e., the Utes) as to ceding this portion of the Reservation, and as to their quietly remaining at this agency, than too many council talk offers at present. All that is necessary to affect a treaty with these Utes is the restoration of Ouray's son to them, and giving authority to Mr. Brunot to offer them a fair consideration.[49] What Adams was referring to were the orders issued for the troops at Fort Garland to oust miners from the reservation.[50] These orders to oust the trespassers were soon modified to say no force should be used against the trespassers.[51] Adams' April report turned out to be the first document later cited by the Secretary of Interior in responding to a December 8, 1879 Senate Resolution calling for a report on mining camps on the Ute Reservation, and on efforts made to remove those camps.[52]

Later, Adams said that the Ute chiefs no longer wanted to go to Washington, but were prepared to discuss at Los Pinos a possible cession agreement. Adams asserted that Brunot's promise to help get Ouray's son back had made the Utes want Brunot to come to them with proposals for a cession treaty.[53] Brunot had been present at Los Pinos in August, 1872 when McCook tried but failed to get the Utes to agree to a cession. In June, Adams and Ouray went to the Cheyenne Agency in eastern Colorado to meet privately with Brunot. Adams told Washington afterwards that the meeting had gone well, that Brunot had offered to help return Ouray's son to him, and that Ouray had promised Brunot to use his influence with his tribe to get a cession agreement accepted.[54] This son of Ouray had been captured by the Arapaho Indians some 10 years earlier on the Republican River, and was still missing.[55]

---

49.   Letter Adams to the CIA, May 2, 1873, Senate Executive Document 29 (46-2) Serial Set 1882. The Brunot here was head of Grant's Board of Indian Commissioners.

50.   Telegram Adjutant General R. Williams, Headquarters, Department of the Missouri, Fort Leavenworth, Kansas, to the Commandant at Fort Garland, May 16,1873, Senate Executive Document 29 (46-2) Serial Set 1882.

51.   Telegram Adjutant General R. Williams, Headquarters, Department of the Missouri, Fort Leavenworth, Kansas, to the Commandant at Fort Garland, May 17,1873, Senate Executive Document 29 (46-2) Serial Set 1882.

52.   Letter Schurz to the President of the Senate, January 7, 1880, Senate Executive Document 29 (46-2) Serial Set 1882.

53.   Letter Adams to the CIA, May 7,1873, NARA M234, Roll 203.

54.   Letter Adams to the CIA, June 27, 1873, NARA M234, Roll 203.

55.   Record of the Commission to Negotiate with the Utes, CIA, 1873, pp. 83 to 113.

Early in August, Adams reported that about 1,800 Utes had gathered at the Los Pinos agency to await Brunot.[56] Brunot reached Los Pinos on September 6, 1873, missing, either by chance or choice, the military escort which had awaited him at Fort Garland. Despite his advance work, Brunot found that getting final agreement on the cession was not easy. From September 6 to 12, he met daily with the Utes in council. A Tabeguache headman, Chief Shavano, forcefully attacked the surveys then being run (by Robert C. Darling under contract to the General Land Office) that were showing the 107th meridian lay west of the current agency location. Shavano charged that the surveyors' lines violated the treaty, and maintained that the Cochetopa Mountains were the true boundary of the reservation on the east. The Indians spent much of the time in council by themselves. Finally, on the seventh day, Saturday, September 13, Ouray and the principal men came to Brunot and expressed a conditional willingness to sign an agreement. They demanded that headmen of the different bands, accompanied by the Secretary of the Commission, visit the area to be ceded. If this area proved to be mountainous mining land and not farming land, then all the Indians would sign. If the reverse case was true, then the agreement would not get the consent of the necessary 3/4 of the tribe.[57] In the end, enough Utes did sign. Since very few of the Utes had shown any interest in farming, this emphasis on farming land was surprising. Perhaps what the Utes really were concerned about was retaining watered lowlands where they could pasture their stock and spend the harsh winters.

Under the so-called Brunot Agreement there reached, the Utes would give up a central chunk of their reservation reaching from the 107th meridian on the east to just short of the Utah line on the west. The chunk began from 15 miles north of the New Mexico line and ran to 10 miles north of the 38th parallel, a distance of about 60 miles. The area thus carved out for surrender includes the present towns of Cortez on the west and Pagosa Springs on the east. The future towns of Ouray, Telluride, Silverton, Durango and Lake City were within the ceded area. The Brunot boundaries seem clear, but just as a dispute had arisen over the eastern boundary of the 1868 reservation along the 107th meridian, so a problem would arise as with the northern boundary of the ceded area.

The United States had originally wanted to get the Utes to give up the 15 mile wide strip that the Utes kept just north of the Colorado-New Mexico line. This strip was earmarked in the Brunot Agreement as a future home for the Muache,

---

56. Letter Adams to the CIA, August 16, 1873, NARA M234, Roll 203.
57. Record of the Commission to Negotiate with the Utes, CIA, 1873, pp. 83 to 113.

Capote and Wiminuche bands. In Article IV, Washington promised at some time to put up buildings in this strip and establish an agency to serve those bands, who thus won out on their long refusal to join the Tabeguache at Los Pinos. Washington agreed to pay the entire Ute tribe $25,000 a year, and to allow Utes to hunt in the surrendered land "as long the game lasts." Over 100 years later, a hunter from the Mountain Ute Reservation tested this latter provision. Arrested by Colorado Game Wardens for killing a deer in the strip without a Colorado hunting license, the arrested man cited the Brunot treaty and was freed by the Colorado court.[58]

In Article VI of the agreement, the government undertook to pay Chief Ouray $1,000 a year for ten years, provided that he remained, in the words of the agreement, the Ute's "Principal Chief." Was Washington by this trying to influence the Utes' choice of their leader? This provision for payment to Ouray may not have been widely known; some Indians later claimed they would not have signed the cession agreement if they had been aware of this provision.[59]

In gratitude for their help in getting the Brunot agreement accepted, Adams escorted a delegation of Ute chiefs to Washington in October, 1873. He requested the Office of Indian Affairs to put them up in one of the better hotels close to the White House and Treasury.[60] At this time, the Office of Indian Affairs gave some thought to moving the Los Pinos Agency to lower ground along the Gunnison River. On his return to Colorado, Adams sent Washington a cost estimate for this move[61] but nothing came of this idea while he was agent at Los Pinos.

The Secretary of the Interior transmitted the Brunot agreement to the President early in January, 1874, preparatory to Senate ratification, and sent a courtesy copy to the Speaker of the House since money was involved. The Senate ratified it on April 29, 1874,[62] making no changes. The 1874 report of the Commissioner of Indian Affairs gave the Indian population at the Los Pinos Agency as

58. Nancy Wood, *When Buffalo Range the Mountains*, Doubleday and Co, Garden City, N. Y., 1980, p. 84
59. Report of Maj. Gen. Edward Hatch, Head of the Commission to Negotiate with the Utes, Senate Exec. Doc. 29 (46-2), Serial Set 1882, p. 78.
60. Telegram Adams to the acting CIA, Oct. 14, 1873, NARA M234, Roll 204.
61. Adams' successor made certain recommendations to Washington about this, and oversaw moving the Los Pinos Agency from the Cochetopa area to the Uncompahgre River.
62. 18 Stat. 36.

2,703, and recommended that the Agency be moved, at last, to the real Los Pinos River.[63]

In the spring of 1874, Adams became concerned at the influx of settlers from New Mexico, and wrote to Washington calling attention to Article 5 of the 1868 Treaty providing that "no persons not authorized shall ever be permitted to pass over, settle upon, or reside in, the territory left as their reservation." Adams urged strong action "to keep faith with the Indians."[64] When the Secretary of Interior asked Secretary of War Belknap to use military force to evict the trespassers, Belknap replied that Indian Service officials should first try on their own to get the trespassers out, and if this failed, those officials could ask the Commandant at Fort Garland for troops.[65] As it turned out, Adams found that the warning against trespassing worked which Washington had authorized. Adams said that with few exceptions, the people to whom he gave notice did not wish to trespass upon Indian lands, and said they had done so only in ignorance.

Adams did not at this time anticipate any need to call on the military authorities. But he saw a problem: "I myself do not exactly know the lines of the reservation, as the maps of this part of the territory cannot be relied upon."[66] Adams was understandably distressed when he learned that General Land Office contractor Darling had surveyed the eastern boundary of the reservation, without any notice having been given to him.[67] He renewed his request for information on that survey when, in mid-1874, a group of about 30 men, calling themselves the Gunnison Town Company incorporated under the law of Colorado Territory, settled on lands on the Gunnison River near the agency cattle camp. The men claimed that this camp was outside the reservation, according to maps they had obtained from Washington. Adams was sure they were trespassing on the reservation, but without maps could not prove it.[68] Full information on the Darling survey reached Los Pinos only after Adams had left his post. When the Darling survey information did come to Los Pinos, Adams' successor reported to Washington that the Indians were distressed at where the Darling survey placed the eastern

---

63. CIA, 1874, p. 52

64. Letter Adams to the CIA, February 21, 1874, NARA M234, Roll 204.

65. Letter Secretary of War to the Secretary of Interior, March 18, 1874, NARA M234, Roll 204.

66. Letter Adams to the CIA, May 4,1874, NARA M234, Roll 204.

67. *ibid.* But Chief Shavano showed during the negotiations with Brunot that he was aware of how Darling's line was turning out.

68. Letter Adams to the CIA, June 1,1874, NARA M234, Roll 204. The Army Corps of Engineers also carried out a survey the area in 1873.

reservation boundary, and also claimed that they had not understood that the reservation boundaries were to be straight lines. They had expected all bottom land would be left to them.[69]

Charles Adams was forced out of the Indian Service in July, 1874, unceremoniously. Action had been underway for some time in Washington to send a true Unitarian to Los Pinos as agent,[70] but Adams was never informed of this.[71] On July 30, 1874, his last day as Agent, Adams wrote a letter to the Commissioner of Indian Affairs which showed his disappointment at how he was treated: "I depart from this agency and the Indians through no fault of my own. If I have engendered the enmity of parties in authority and accusations have been brought against me, I have not been granted the privilege of defending myself. I have no fault to find, only this I know, that the Indians are sorry to see me leave this agency."[72]

It is not clear why Adams was treated so shabbily. Possibly it was because he had been appointed Indian Agent at Los Pinos under false pretenses. Governor McCook, a friend of President Grant, had gotten Adams the appointment as Indian agent at Los Pinos by representing him as a Unitarian.[73] Adams was actually a Catholic. On being dismissed as Agent at Los Pinos, Adams became a postal inspector. After the 1879 Meeker revolt, Adams would be called back into service. Working well with Ouray, Adams would do much to held down bloodshed in that incident. In 1880, President Hayes appointed Adams United States Minister to Bolivia. As such, he acted as U.S. mediator at talks between Bolivia and Chile to settle one or the periodic conflicts between those countries. Adams left the Foreign Service in 1882, again to be a postal inspector. President Cleveland, anathema in Colorado after pushing through the 1893 repeal of the Sherman Silver Purchase Act, dismissed Adams from the postal service on charges of "gross partisanship." Adams was killed in August, 1895 in an explosion at Denver's Gumry Hotel.[74]

---

69. Letter Bond to the CIA, August 3, 1874, NARA M234, Roll 294.

70. Henry F. Bond received his Presidential Commission as Agent at Los Pinos in June, per letter Bond to the CIA, June 27, 1874, NARA M234, Roll 204. Since such a commission can be issued only with the advice and consent of the Senate, action to replace Adams must have been underway for some time.

71. Telegram Adams to the CIA, July 9, 1874, NARA M234, Roll 204.

72. Letter Adams to the CIA, July 30, 1874, NARA M234, Roll 204.

73. Keller, *op. cit.*, p. 65.

74. Allen Johnson, *Dictionary of American Biography*, New York, Charles Scribners' Sons, 1964, Volume 1, p. 39.

3

The Los Pinos Agency Moves West

Henry F. Bond, Adams' designated successor, was a true Unitarian. Bond like Trask was a graduate of Harvard College and of the Harvard Divinity School. Bond officially took over as agent at Los Pinos on July 30, 1874. A few days later, Bond wrote to the Commissioner of Indian Affairs that he had received the long sought field notes of the Darling survey of 1873, and that Indians were not at all happy with the boundary lines shown.[1] A week later, he chastised the Office of Indian Affairs for sending to Los Pinos a circular request for all agencies to report how many Indians were employed in agriculture, the occupation Washington wanted Indians everywhere to take up. Bond wrote that he failed to see that this requirement applied to his agency. Los Pinos he wrote was located in high mountains, and the growing season was very short, if such existed at all. There was frost every month of the year, and that no attempt to raise crops would be successful. He opined that, at most, a few Indians might be employed in herding cattle at the herding camp on the Gunnison River. Noting that the 1868 treaty provided that the government would give the Indians food until they were capable of sustaining themselves, he asserted that they could never sustain themselves around the agency as then situated. He suggested that the Uncompahgre valley, where Ouray and a large number of Utes regularly spent winters, would be a good site to which to move the agency.[2] In contrast to Trask, Bond did not see his job as converting the Utes to Christianity. But Bond kept up his ties with the Unitarian Church in Boston which had recommended him for the position as Indian agent, asking them to name a physician for Los Pinos when that position became vacant later.[3]

---

1. Letter Bond to the CIA, August 3, 1874, NARA M234, Roll 204.
2. Letter Bond to the CIA, August 10, 1874, NARA M234, Roll 204.

In October, 1874, not long after Bond took over, Ouray and about a thousand of the Indians from Los Pinos went to Denver, preparatory to hunting buffalo on the plains east of the city. About 500 Utes from the White River agency joined their brethren in Denver for this hunt. Agent Bond followed Ouray to Denver, where he distributed provisions to the Indians. Bond wrote that buffalo had been reported about 80 miles east of Denver, and that he did not anticipate any trouble in the Ute's hunt.[4] Bond was off the mark with this optimism. He had left Denver before the Utes who went on the buffalo hunt returned around the end of November and again encamped near Denver. The Utes told Special Agent Thompson in Denver that they had fought with the Sioux, capturing about 300 horses, property of the latter. The chiefs told Thompson that they would spend the remainder of the winter near Canyon City, and that the main band would not go back to the reservation until spring.[5] Ouray later defended the Utes' action against the Sioux, and said it would be a great injustice for the Special Agent to force the Utes to return the captured horses.[6]

In view of Ute anger over the results of the survey of the eastern reservation boundary, Bond in December, 1874 recommended to Washington that, when an official survey was run of the boundaries of the land to be taken back by the United States under the Brunot Treaty, representative Indians take part in the survey in some fashion.[7] Bond was prescient in anticipating trouble over demarcation of the Brunot Treaty boundary lines.

Washington initially thought of moving the Los Pinos agency to a lower altitude close to the site of the agency cattle camp, north of where the Gunnison Town Company was building its settlement. Bond had suggested reserving strips three miles wide on each side of the Gunnison and Tomichi to a distance of 10 miles west from the presumed eastern line of the reservation. He noted that there were already some settlers within these limits who would have to be removed, but thought it would be best to do this sooner rather than later. When the location of the 107th meridian became known, Bond told Washington that the survey had put the cattle camp four or five miles east of the reservation boundary. Bond said that Chief Ouray had consented to moving the cattle camp 15 miles further west

---

3.   Letter Secretary of the American Unitarian Association to the Secretary of the Interior, Nov. 13, 1874, NARA M234, Roll 204.

4.   Letter Bond to the CIA, October 18,1874, NARA M234, Roll 204.

5.   Letter Denver Indian Agent Thompson to the CIA, December 4, 1874, NARA M234, Roll 204.

6.   Letter Thompson to the CIA, December 16, 1874, NARA M234, Roll 204.

7.   Letter Bond to the CIA, December 22, 1874, NARA M234, Roll 204.

down the Gunnison River.[8] In December, 1874, Bond sent the Commissioner of Indian Affairs a tracing from Hayden's latest map on which he marked the location of the agency cattle camp as on the Gunnison River north of its junction with Tomichi Creek. Bond pointed out that this cattle camp, like the agency itself, was outside the Ute reservation. Bond again said that the agency might best be moved to the Uncompahgre Valley, where he thought the Utes could live the year round and be taught agriculture and the arts necessary for reservation life.[9] Washington did not immediately accept this Uncompahgre Valley proposal, perhaps in part because the Utes usually resisted being moved westward.

Later, at Washington's request for his recommendation, Bond came in with a proposal for moving the agency a short distance to the Cebolla Valley and the adjacent Powderhorn Valley. Bond assured Washington that these valleys were within the reservation boundaries.[10] He opined that these valleys were about as far from the present agency location as the Utes would easily accept.[11] At Washington's direction, Bond went to the Utes' wintering site near Canon City, where he asked Ouray if the Indians would consent to moving to the Cebolla-Powderhorn site. Ouray said that he would discuss the matter with his chiefs, and give Bond the answer in May when the Indians returned to the agency.[12] But Washington was in a hurry, and authorized Bond to move the agency to the Cebolla-Powderhorn site without waiting for further input from the Indians.[13]

Something had happened to change Chief Ouray's mind about moving the agency. In May, Bond told Washington that Ouray was now in favor of moving the agency to the Uncompahgre Valley, and was so convinced this was appropriate that he did not think it necessary to hold a council to get full agreement of all the Indians. Bond therefore said he was going with Ouray to that valley to choose a suitable site.[14] Bond had long thought the Uncompahgre Valley was the best location for the agency, having the right soil and climate.

The Office of Indian Affairs in Washington seemed to be poorly informed about how things were in Colorado, and Bond had to tell Washington that the newly-constructed San Juan Toll Road encroached on the Ute reservation, run-

---

8. Letter Bond to the CIA, December 12, 1874, NARA M234, Roll 204

9. Letter Bond to the CIA, January 11, 1875, NARA M234, Roll 205.

10. Letter Bond to the CIA, Feb. 9, 1875, NARA M234, Roll 206. Powderhorn post office was clearly within the Reservation.

11. Letter Bond to the CIA, Feb. 9,1875, NARA M234, Roll 205.

12. Letter Bond to the CIA, March 17,1875, NARA M234, Roll 205.

13. Letter Bond to the CIA, April 6, 1875, NARA M234, Roll 205.

14. Letter Bond to the CIA, May 18,1875, NARA M234, Roll 205.

ning for 15 to 20 miles through the reservation from a point on the eastern boundary about seven miles north of the northern boundary of the Brunot Treaty cession area. Bond said that determining the degree of encroachment would have to await the forthcoming survey of the exact area ceded under the Brunot Treaty; he had already warned the builders of the road that they might have to move the route.[15] Bond also warned the Commissioner of Indian Affairs that the Indians were much annoyed that they had not been paid either the annuities due under the 1868 treaty, nor what they were due under the Brunot Treaty ratified in 1874. Bond urged that the money due the Utes under the Brunot Treaty be paid to them by the April, 1875 anniversary of the Brunot Treaty ratification.[16] The first annuity payment was not until in 1876, however.

The move of the Los Pinos agency to the Uncompahgre River began in July, 1875,[17] but took time to complete. Bond did not officially open the agency at the latter site until November 29, 1875.[18] Bond's September 30, 1876 submission to the Commissioner of Indian Affairs for the 1876 Annual Report detailed the move to the new location. Bond wrote that "the move will keep the Indians nearer the heart of reservation in a country where successful cultivation of the soil is possible, where they can reach the ration house at all seasons of the year and be more frequently under the eye of the agent. The present location is about 6,000 feet above sea level vs. 9,000 at the old location. The new site is within two miles of the head of what is known as the Uncompahgre Valley.... From high points on the range of mountains 15 miles south of here, the Valley is said to look very charming and attractive. The extra labor for the moving the agency was hired on July 14. The old agency was not on the reservation and was otherwise objectionable. On the 17th July, we began to move the sawmill. The agency farmer and a band of hired men took three weeks, four ox wagons and one mule wagon, to reach the new mill site, a distance of little over 90 miles. It was necessary to build a great part of the road. The main work at the new site was to dig the ditch over a half-mile long, in hard cement-like gravel on the edge of a bluff. The contract for erecting the buildings was let on August 12, with the work to be completed by August 25 unless delayed by lack of lumber."[19]

The Annual Report of the Commissioner of Indian Affairs for 1875 (probably finished in October) noted that of the 2,900 Utes on the reservation in Colorado

15.   Letter Bond to the CIA, January 4,1875, NARA M234, Roll 205.
16.   Letter Bond to the CIA, Feb. 3,1875, NARA M234, Roll 206.
17.   Letter Bond to the CIA, July 23,1875, NARA M234, Roll 205.
18.   Letter Bond to the CIA, Sept. 30, 1876, CIA, 1876, p. 18.
19.   Letter Bond to the CIA, Sept. 30, 1876, CIA, 1876, p. 18.

at the White River and Los Pinos Agencies, only 19 families had made any attempt at farming. The Colorado Utes were still dissatisfied with lines of the Brunot Treaty of 1873, by which they claimed they were being deprived of large areas of farming lands. They insisted this was contrary to their intentions and their expressed declarations at the time of the treaty signing. This 1875 Report erroneously said that the Los Pinos agency was in the process of removal from its location on the "Grand River outside the reservation to the Los Pinos River." If this shows anything, it is how little the Office of the Commissioner knew about Colorado geography. The new Los Pinos agency was on a tributary of the Gunnison, not the Grand, namely the Uncompahgre, not the Los Pinos, River.

Bond's contribution to the 1875 Annual Report of the Commissioner of Indian Affairs was dated Los Pinos, September 16, 1875. He complained that "counting the Indians is as hard as counting a swarm of bees on the wing. They travel over the country like the deer which they hunt. Even to register those whom you see would be difficult, for when you ask their names, 'no name' is the common reply." He pointed out that the cattle belonging to the agency, numbering over 900, cost the government a great deal to keep. He said that the herd, originally wild Texas cattle now somewhat improved by the introduction of a few American bulls, were entirely unfit for the original purpose, namely domestic use. He said that probably only a few could ever be trained to become good milkers, and noted that not a single cow had been taken by the Indians for family use. In July, 1876, Bond went back to the old agency site to try to round up Ute cattle left at the former range near Gunnison. Although he had 5 men, he found the cattle too wild to be caught. He asked permission to offer $5 per head to anyone who would catch and deliver the cattle to the new agency site.[20] He also suggested to Washington that since it cost the government a great deal to keep the cattle, paying for herders and otherwise, why not turn the cattle over to the Indians?

Bond reported that four exploring survey parties had visited the Los Pinos agency during the year, two from the Hayden expedition, one under James Miller surveying the Brunot cession line, and one headed by Army Lt. Marshall working under Lt. George Wheeler.[21] Why so many different survey groups? Because several different agencies were sponsoring such expeditions. Miller worked for the General Land Office. The Army Officers had been sent out by the Corps of Engineers. Hayden, who bore the title of United States Geologist, worked under the

---

20. Letter Bond to the CIA, July 17,1876, NARA M234, Roll 206.
21. Letter Bond to the CIA, Sept. 16,1875, CIA, 1875, pp. 232-234.

direction of Secretary of Interior. By 1878, Congress had become concerned about duplication in exploring and mapping the West, and asked the National Academy of Sciences for its recommendations. The Academy rendered its opinion in November, 1878 and advised bringing all surveys and explorations of the Territories under the Department of the Interior.[22] Defending his turf, the Secretary of War told Congress that the Corps of Engineers surveys were producing useful information and that steps were now being taken to prevent any overlap in areas covered by expeditions sponsored by the War Department and the Department of Interior.[23] However, Congress cut off War Department funding for exploration west of the 100th Meridian, and made the Department of Interior solely responsible for this task as the Academy had recommended. The Wheeler explorations did bring the Library of Congress some of the few extant photographs taken of Ute Indians in the field in the 1880's.

In his September letter, Bond noted that one Hayden party had been driven away from Sierra La Sal in Utah and back into Colorado. After talking to Ouray, the Hayden Party decided that their attackers were from a renegade band of Paiutes. Although those outlaws acknowledged allegiance to no one, Ouray ordered them to appear at the Los Pinos agency. They did come in but offered no good explanation for the attack The Paiutes did express a desire to be friendly and kindly treated by Ouray's Indians. Bond gave them presents and expected no further trouble from them. This incident showed that Ouray's influence was not limited by state boundaries.

In November, 1875 Bond requested that a military post be placed along the Uncompahgre River below the new Los Pinos site to deter settlers from trespassing on the reservation. He reported that a group of settlers has camped at the agency, planning to go through the reservation to the headwaters of the Uncompahgre River to establish a town outside the reservation.[24] Bond feared this town (called Ouray) would become a source of friction between Utes and whites. In March, 1876, evidently responding to criticism from Washington about his lack of progress in developing Indian agriculture and his hiring of non-Indian labor, Bond said that in engaging outside labor to cut hay at the old agency site, he was merely following the practice of his predecessors. And he said

---

22.   Letter Marsh to the President of the Senate, November 26, 1878, Senate Miscellaneous Document 9 (45-3), Serial Set 1833.
23.   Letter Secretary of War to the Speaker of the House, May 10, 1878, House Miscellaneous Document 88 (45-2), Serial Set 1809.
24.   Letter Bond to the CIA, November 11, 1875, House Executive Document 90 (42-3), Serial Set 65.

he was ready to try growing oats at the new agency, if Washington would supply combines.[25]

Nepotism was evidently not a problem in the 1870's. Bond had put his son, Frederick, on the agency payroll as a miller. At the end of 1875 and in early 1876, Frederick was employed at the old agency site to safeguard supplies and equipment left there.[26] Bond not only hired his son but also followed Adams' practice in putting his wife, Pamela, on the agency payroll as a teacher. Washington did not like this arrangement, not on nepotism grounds, but because the Los Pinos school then had few or no Indian students. The Office on Indian Affairs would pay the salary of a teacher only if there were Indian children in the school. At Los Pinos, the only students regularly attending were four children of agency employees. Bond assured Washington that the number of Indian scholars at the school would increase.[27] Earlier, in February, 1875, Bond did in fact stop paying his wife for teaching. She continued, without pay, to instruct the one regular student, a child of an agency employee. Bond started his wife's salary again in late April, 1875 when some Indians families showed up and put three Indian children in school.[28]

By the summer of 1876, steps were being taken to sell the buildings at the old agency site. Bond realized that not all supplies and equipment had been cleared out from the old buildings and brought to the Uncompahgre River. He told Washington that he would send agency ox teams back to the old site to pick up useful supplies, but would release any other supplies to the Indians. He urged that the government retain control of the warehouse at the old site for storing property.[29]

Getting things delivered to the agency at its new location in the Uncompahgre Valley was difficult. When the agency moved, some of the stock on hand was left at the old location, where Bond had left his son in charge. Contractors hired to make deliveries to the agency at its new location, whether through ignorance of the change or in willful refusal to haul goods to new, more distant location, left their cargo at the old agency where they got son Frederick to receipt for it.[30]

25. Letter Bond to the CIA, March 6,1876, NARA M234, Roll 206.
26. Certificate of Frederick W. Bond, March 9,1876, NARA M234, Roll 206.
27. Letter Bond to the CIA, May 17,1876, NARA M234, Roll 206.
28. Letter Bond to the CIA, May 4,1875, NARA M234, Roll 205.
29. After Bond was replaced as Indian agent at Los Pinos, the CIA disapproved this sale, apparently on the grounds that the buildings were sold too cheaply. Bond then protested the Commissioner's disapproval. See Bond letter to the CIA, Jan. 19,1877, NARA M234, Roll 207.

Agent Bond successfully maintained that his son had no authorization to discharge the freighters from their contract to deliver the supplies to the new agency location. Later that year, Senator Henry Teller introduced a bill in Congress to pay the freight companies anyway.[31] Bond told Washington that the cost of the moving goods and supplies to the Uncompahgre River would less if a proper road existed. He wrote that private enterprise might build a road part way to the agency site if the President granted the necessary land. However, he said that private enterprise was not likely to build a wagon road all the way to agency, and urged that government funds be appropriated for building a road.[32]

The Los Pinos agency at its new site did not, as hoped, place the Tabeguache out of the way of incoming settlers and miners. In fact, the Uncompahgre River site placed the Tabeguache closer than ever before to an area of real conflict, namely the tract known as Uncompahgre Park. When James W. Miller, under contract to the General Land Office, surveyed the course of northern line of the area ceded by the Utes in the Brunot Treaty, he apparently did not find the feature identified in the Brunot Treaty as Uncompahgre Park.[33] The treaty had provided "that if any part of the Uncompahgre Park shall be found to extend the south of the north line of said country, the same is not intended to be concluded therein, and is thereby reserved and retained as a portion of the Ute reservation." There is some justification for Miller's failure to find the Park, as it is more like an opening between two valleys than a true mountain park. The Utes may have wanted Uncompahgre Park primarily for the hot spring there, but to whites in the town of Ouray, the area seemed a good place to grow food crops and graze animals.

Squatters in fact put up houses and started agricultural operations in Uncompahgre Park when Surveyor Miller made no diversion in his boundary line to leave Uncompahgre Park in the reservation. The General Land Office maintained that neither the Indians nor the Los Pinos agent went with Miller when he made his survey, so he had found nothing meeting the description of a park.[34] When he became aware of Miller's conclusions, Bond warned Washington of trouble over this tract. He suggested that Miller not be paid for his work until he had re-surveyed the line, making the deviation required under the

30. Letter Bond to the CIA, Feb. 8,1876, NARA M234, Roll 206.
31. Senate bill S. 1220, 44th Congress, Second Session, Feb. 3, 1877.
32. Letter Bond to the CIA, June 2,1876, NARA M234, Roll 206.
33. Letter General Land Office to the CIA, July 24,1876, Senate Executive Document No. 29 (46-2), Serial Set 1882.
34. Letter Bond to the CIA, December 18,1876, NARA M234, Roll 206.

Brunot Treaty so as to leave Uncompahgre Park to the Indians.[35] President Grant showed sympathy for the Indians by issuing an Executive Order on August 17, 1876 transferring to them the so-called Four Mile Tract containing the hot spring. The tract, as described in the Executive Order, began at the 53rd mile post on the north border of the 1875 Miller survey, then ran south four miles; thence east four miles; thence north four miles to the north line; thence west to the place of the beginning. But Grant's Executive Order would not end forever the battle over Uncompahgre Park.

Also in August, 1876, Bond found it necessary to defend himself from complaints made to Washington, apparently by Chief Ouray. These focused on Bond's opposition to Ouray's efforts to build a house for himself on reservation property but not right at the Agency. Bond admitted that he had tried to make Ouray build his house close to the agency, since Bond wanted to be able to call on Ouray at a moment's notice. Bond said in this letter that because Ouray had already built adobe walls for his house well away from the Agency buildings, using hired Mexican labor, Bond would no longer put obstacles in the way of Ouray's house project.[36]

Henry Bond's appointment as Indian Agent at Los Pinos ended September 30, 1876. From Saguache, Colorado, in October, he wrote the Office of Indian Affairs that his future address would be Wakefield, Massachusetts.[37] Early in 1877 from Wakefield, Bond answered criticism of his sale of the agency buildings at the old site, asserting that everything connected with the sale had been done in accordance with the letter and spirit of the instructions from the Commissioner of Indian Affairs. Although the amount derived from the sale turned out to be exceedingly small, Bond said that there was nothing whatsoever in the advertising or the timing of the sale which precluded the sale price from having been larger.[38] In Massachusetts, Bond became pastor of Unitarian churches at Northboro and Nantucket. For a period around 1880, he was in business in Boston. The 1880 Census shows him as a 60 year old leather dealer living on Tremont Street in Boston, with his wife Margaret and 28 year old son Frederick, also a leather dealer.[39] Bond's time with Indians was not yet over.

---

35.   Letter Bond to the CIA, May 24, 1876, Senate Executive Document No. 29 (46-2), Serial Set 1882.

36.   Letter Bond to the CIA, Aug. 10,1876, NARA M234, Roll 206.

37.   Letter Bond to the CIA, Oct. 25,1876, NARA M234, Roll 206.

38.   Letter Bond to the CIA, Jan. 19, 1877, NARA M234, Roll 207.

39.   1880 Census, Roll 558, Enumeration District 714, Sheet 12, line 40.

At the beginning of 1886, a Unitarian group decided to raise funds to establish a manual training school on some western Indian reservation. Who better to send to do this than former Indian agent Henry Bond and his former teacher wife? The Bonds first looked for a site in Utah, to which their old friends, the Tabeguache, had been banished, but ultimately chose a location on the Crow reservation in Montana, close to the Big Horn River just south of Custer. Relying on donations, the Bonds got the buildings put up and achieved a modest enrollment. Officially the school was called the Industrial School for Indians, but it was also known locally as the "Bond Mission." By 1890, with Henry now 70, the Bonds felt worn out and returned to Massachusetts, taking up residence in West Newton. The government took over the Bond school in the mid-1890's.[40] Henry Bond died in 1907 while on vacation in New Hampshire.[41]

Bond's successor, Willard D. Wheeler, was nominated by the Unitarians in August, 1876 to be the agent at Los Pinos.[42] Formally appointed on September 14, 1876, Wheeler was quick to arrive at Los Pinos, since he was already serving as agent at the White River Agency. Wheeler's name appeared on a September 25, 1876 advertisement seeking proposals for delivering certain supplies to the new Los Pinos agency, although the record shows he did not officially assume charge of the Agency until the end of that month.[43]

Wheeler soon came to admire Chief Ouray, describing Ouray "without question the most intelligent and the most progressive Indian of the whole world." Evidently during Wheeler's tenure, Ouray managed to finish his house, the construction of which Bond had opposed. Somewhat inconsistently, Wheeler said that no public funds were used in building the house, while noting that the agency carpenter and other personnel had helped in the project. Wheeler also praised Ouray for having developed a farm where he had raised about four acres of potatoes, a respectable field of wheat, some corn, and a variety of vegetables. Wheeler said Ouray's example might stimulate other members of the tribe to try farming.[44]

Wheeler's big problem was the same problem that had so troubled Bond: the influx of whites into the Ute reservation. The problem of the settlers in Uncompahgre Park, which the Brunot Treaty had reserved for the Indians, was a

40.   Margery Pease, _The Montana Industrial School, 1886-1897_, privately published by the Author in 1986.
41.   _Christian Register_, Boston, Sept. 29, 1907.
42.   Letter Shippen to the CIA, August 23, 1876, NARA M808, Roll 13.
43.   Newspaper clipping, Sept. 25, 1876, M234, Roll 207.
44.   Letter Wheeler to the CIA, October 29, 1877, CIA, 1877, p. 43.

particular plague for the agent at Los Pinos. Wheeler wrote Washington that to placate the Indians, he had told them the settlers would leave the Park in the spring. Wheeler said that he had spoken to the settlers, most but not all of whom promised to leave in the spring.[45] After Grant's 1876 Executive Order restored the Park to the Utes, Wheeler in March, 1877 gave written notice to the squatters to leave, setting a deadline of April 1, 1877.[46] Wheeler told Washington in April, 1877 that a few of the Uncompahgre Park settlers did leave voluntarily, but that the others had made it clear they would not leave unless driven out by military force. Senator Teller then intervened, writing to Interior Secretary Interior Secretary Schurz from his law office in Central City.[47] Teller referred to affidavits from a number of settlers in Uncompahgre Park, asserting that they had gone into Uncompahgre Park in good faith after Miller's survey line placed it outside the Ute reservation.[48] Replying to Teller, Interior Secretary Schurz moved the deadline for the squatters to leave back to October 1, 1877, ostensibly to give the settlers time to harvest crops they may have planted.[49] Squatters planting crops in Uncompahgre Park were not Wheeler's only problem. He also had trouble with settlers allowing their cattle to roam on reservation land, overrunning the best land where the agency kept its own cattle and had built a cabin for the hired herder. He told Washington that some did this deliberately, so that during the spring round up, they could claim agency cattle as their own. The agency herd was allowed to run wild and was not branded.[50]

In his submission for the 1877 Annual Report of the Commissioner of Indian Affairs, Wheeler said he believed that many of the settlers in Uncompahgre Park really wanted to provoke the Indians into the use of force, believing that the end result of such bloodshed would be the ouster of all the Utes from Colorado.[51] In Ouray, citizens reported organized two military companies of militia and

---

45. Letter Wheeler to the CIA, December 9, 1876, Senate Exec. Doc. 29 (46-2), Serial Set 1882.

46. Letter Wheeler to the CIA, April 9, 1877, Senate Executive Document No. 29 (46-2), Serial Set 1882.

47. Letter Teller to Interior Secretary Schurz, June 13, 1878, Senate Executive Document No. 29 (46-2), Serial Set 1882.

48. Many protests from Ouray County dated September, 1877, in NARA M234, Roll 207.

49. Letter Interior Secretary Schurz to the CIA, Oct. 19,1877, Senate Executive Document No. 29 (46-2), Serial Set 1882.

50. Letter Wheeler to the CIA, January 2, 1877, Senate Executive Document No. 29 (46-2), Serial Set 1882.

51. Letter Wheeler to the CIA, October 29, 1877. CIA, 1877, p. 43.

obtained a hundred guns from the state armory in Denver for the use in fighting the Utes of Los Pinos. Fortunately, cooler heads prevailed.

What was Ute Indian life like in 1877? For one thing, most of the Tabeguache did not copy Ouray by living in a house. They remained in teepees, no doubt because they continued to go on hunts. Even as late as 1877, the majority showed up at the agency only on distribution days. Agent Wheeler recommended that goods be distributed only every 10 days, so as to discourage the Utes from giving up hunting, which still supplied much of their material needs.[52]

Interior Secretary Carl Interior Secretary Schurz decided early in September to find a replacement for Wheeler, reacting to complaints about him made by many officials and residents of Ouray County.[53] A group of officials of Ouray County had sent an undated letter (presumably around September, 1878) to the Secretary charging that Wheeler had been giving spirits to the Indians, and keeping spirits in Indian territory contrary to U.S. law. Ouray resident Josiah Fogg wrote Washington that Wheeler was disliked there because he was "too liberal and drank too much whiskey."[54] Interior Secretary Schurz then asked the Unitarians to nominate the replacement for Wheeler.[55] A few months later, on December 3, 1877, Wheeler was replaced as Agent at Los Pinos. Wheeler persisted to the end of his time as Agent at Los Pinos in trying to oust the settlers from Uncompahgre Park. Ironically, on December 3, 1877, the very day his replacement was named, Wheeler wrote to the Commandant at Fort Garland asking for troops to enforce the ouster of the squatters.[56]

---

52. Letter Wheeler to the CIA, October 29, 1877, CIA, 1877, p. 43.
53. NARA M808, Roll 13
54. Letter Fogg to the CIA, Sept. 20, 1878, Senate Exec. Doc. 29 (46-2), Serial Set 1882.
55. Letter Interior Secretary Schurz to the CIA, Sept. 5, 1877, NARA M234, Roll 207.
56. Letter Wheeler to the CIA, December 3, 1877, Senate Executive Document No. 29 (46-2), Serial Set 1882.

4

Problems Along the Uncompahgre

Wheeler's replacement at Los Pinos was Joseph B. Abbott, who took over the agency on January 16, 1878. Abbott advised Washington then that mail communications for him should be sent via Lake City, and telegrams should be sent to the nearest telegraph office, then at Del Norte.[1] Abbott quickly asked Washington for permission to repair what he called the agency's dilapidated buildings.[2] And Abbott very soon took up the fight that Bond and Wheeler had waged against the squatters in Uncompahgre Park, renewing with the Commandant at Fort Garland Wheeler's request for troops.[3] The Commandant replied that he would send troops only on instructions from his own authorities.[4]

The tense situation over Uncompahgre Park gave rise to the idea of putting a military post in the area to prevent hostilities between the Utes and whites. This idea was shot down by General Polk, commanding the Army's Missouri Department at Fort Leavenworth. General Polk did not want a military post in any area not easily accessible to transportation. The Army with its reply gratuitously sent along a lengthy exposition of basic facts about the situation in Colorado, giving the population of Lake City as 2,000 souls and the number of Indians served by the Los Pinos agency also as 2,000.[5] Agent Abbott kept pointing out that whites were settling on the reservation in increasing numbers.[6] A number of Uncompah-

---

1. Letter Abbott to the CIA, Jan. 16,1878, NARA M234, Roll 208.
2. Letter Abbott to the CIA, Jan. 23, 1878, NARA M234, Roll 208.
3. Letter Abbott to the Commandant at Fort Garland, Jan. 24, 1878, NARA M234, Roll 208.
4. Letter Commandant at Fort Garland to Abbott, Jan. 30, 1878, NARA M234, Roll 208.
5. Letter Secretary of War to the Secretary of Interior, March 8,1878, NARA M234, Roll 209.
6. Letter Abbott to the CIA, April 17,1878, NARA M234, Roll 209.

gre Park squatters sent a telegram to Colorado Senators Chaffee and Teller and Representative Patterson stating that agent Abbott and the Army had given them 10 days to leave, at which time troops would remove those remaining and also the post office and stage station.[7] Lt. Rucker of the 9th U.S. Cavalry appeared at Los Pinos in June to assist Abbott in getting the squatters to leave.[8] Meeting with strong resistance from the citizens of Ouray County, Abbott backed off from his threat, and asked Washington for instructions.[9]

While the dispute over settlers in Uncompahgre Park was playing out in Colorado, back in Washington a new effort got underway to consolidate Indian reservations in a number of states, including Colorado. The Office of Indian Affairs prepared a bill providing for this. First idea: reducing the number of agencies would cut on-going government costs. Second idea: consolidating agencies would better protect the Indians' personal and property rights. Third idea: selling the land vacated by the consolidation would raise funds to pay for the removal and resettlement of the Indians. The bill envisioned consolidating 36 existing reservations, encompassing almost 22 million acres of land under the charge of 20 agents, into just 9 reservations, with 4.3 million acres under charge of just 9 agents.[10] This bill was still born.

Colorado Senator Chaffee on February 11, 1878 introduced bill S. 706,[11] calling for negotiations with the Utes to get all of them to move to a new reservation on the White River, giving up the southern part of their reservation. Why choose the White River Agency area for the consolidation? Primarily because no influx of miners was expected there as had happened in the area around the Los Pinos agency. To encourage the Utes to consider moving to the White River, Senator Henry Teller in 1878 suggested that the Office of Indian Affairs begin paying out, at the White River agency, some of the over $50,000 due the Utes under the 1873 Brunot Treaty.[12] Chaffee's bill became the Ute Negotiation Act and came into force on May 3, 1878.[13] The appropriation act signed into law on June 20, 1878[14] contained the sum of $6,000 to pay the expenses of this new Ute Com-

7.   Telegram June 11, 1878, Senate Executive Document No. 29 (46-2), Serial Set 1882.
8.   Letter Abbott to the CIA, June 12,1878, NARA M234, Roll 208.
9.   Letter Abbott to the CIA, June 18,1878, NARA M234, Roll 208.
10.   *Ibid.*, p. IV.
11.   Copy in NARA M234, Roll 208.
12.   Letter Teller to the CIA, May 13,1878, NARA M234, Roll 209.
13.   20 Stat. 48.
14.   20 Stat. 206.

mission, and also money to pay for moving the White River agency to an unspecified new spot and erecting buildings there. Money was also approved for moving the Utes at Cimarron, New Mexico, mostly Muache, to the Ute Reservation in Colorado.

Colonel Edward Hatch, commanding the 9th Cavalry at Santa Fe, New Mexico, was named to head the new Ute Commission to try to carry out this law, that is getting the Utes to give up all of their reservation south of the Grand (now Colorado) River, including Uncompahgre Park. The Commissioner of Indian Affairs gave Hatch $20,000 to pay to those Utes who went along.[15] When the man named to be secretary of Hatch's commission, Stickney, took sick, the Commandant at Fort Garland recommended ex-Governor Morrell of Maine as a replacement, since Morrell just happened to be there on a visit.[16] In the end, the Hatch Commission failed to achieve the objective of getting the Tabeguache and Southern Utes to move to the White River, or at least getting the Tabeguache to give up Uncompahgre Park. The Commission left the West with an understanding that this latter subject would be discussed by a Ute delegation in Washington.

The Muache, Capote, and Wiminuche Utes had long differed with Ouray on where the Los Pinos agency should be located. The Hatch Commission in November, 1878 had succeeded in getting these bands to give up their interest in the existing Ute Reservation by offering them in exchange a new reservation on the headwaters of Chama, Animas, San Juan and Piedra Rivers in Colorado.[17] As he had been instructed, Hatch paid these bands $17 per head for giving up their claims on the 1868 reservation.[18] President Hayes sent Congress Hatch's report on the failure early in 1879.[19]

General John Pope, who attended the talks, gave a negative assessment of the work of the Hatch Commission to his boss, General P. H. Sheridan in Chicago.[20] The Commissioner of Indian Affairs *ex post facto* opined that the Hatch effort was doomed from the outset. He said the existing White River agency was

15. Letter CIA to Hatch, September 25, 1878, Senate Executive Document 29, op. cit., p. 86.

16. Telegram from Department of Missouri, Fort Leavenworth, to Interior Secretary Schurz, Aug. 20, 1878, NARA M234, Roll 209.

17. Letter McFarland to the CIA, Nov. 18, 1878, NARA M234, Roll 209.

18. Hatch Report to the "Commissioner of Interior" (sic), December 27, 1878, Senate Exec. Doc. 29 (46-2), Serial Set 1882.

19. Letter President Hayes to the Senate and House, February 8, 1879, Senate Executive Document 62 (45-3), Serial set 1831. The original handwritten version of the Hatch report is found in NARA M234, Roll 211.

reliably accessible by teams only during two months of the year, and had such poor soil that he could not understand why it had been chosen for locating an agency in the first place. He did note that the White River area was not bad from one point of view: it was not likely to see an influx of whites, "unless the land shall be found to contain minerals."[21] During World War I, the White River area was found to have oil, gas and some of the world's richest oil shale deposits, but in 1878 all this underground wealth was unknown.

Why was the problem of Uncompahgre Park so difficult to solve? Largely unmentioned in the documents is the fact that Uncompahgre Park contained a hot spring, in which Chief Ouray and his wife Chipeta reportedly greatly enjoyed bathing. Some residents of Ouray town interested in mining pointed out that the Indians really wanted only the land around the hot springs and had no interest in the mountainous lands on either side of the four mile square tract reserved for the Utes by President Grant's Executive Order of August 17, 1886. They asked the Secretary of the Interior, in the event an order was issued to oust the squatters from Uncompahgre Park, that this order be worded so as not to cover the mountainous side lands where valuable mineral deposits might exist.[22] A letter one Josiah Fogg, a citizen of Ouray town, wrote to the Commissioner of Indian Affairs in July, 1878, brought out the importance of the hot spring: "when the treaty with the Indians were signed some five years ago, it was understood by the treaty commissioners that the hot springs and Uncompahgre Valley were to be included in the reservation. However, upon running the line and setting the posts this spring, the hot spring and the valley six miles long and averaging 2 miles in width were found to be upon the ceded lands. Upon this being made known to your predecessor, he recommended to President Grant the issuance of the proclamation declaring the four mile square, to include the spring and the larger portion of the Valley, would belong to the reservation and not to the ceded lands. As soon as the government surveyors had run the line and set the points, all or nearly all of the good land in the four mile tract was settled on by settlers, mostly with families. Then the proclamation of President Grant came, and it caused much ill feeling and dissatisfaction."[23]

---

20. Letter General John Pope to General P. H. Sheridan, Sept. 7, 1878, NARA M234, Roll 209.
21. CIA, 1878, p. 188
22. Letter San Juan and San Luis Mining and Smelting Company to the Secretary of Interior, Feb. 1, 1878, Senate Exec. Doc. 29 (46-2), Serial Set 1882.
23. Letter Fogg to the CIA, Sept. 20, 1878, Senate Executive Document 29 (46-2), Serial Set 1882.

In July, 1878, another resident of Ouray, John Outcall, had written to Washington charging Agent Abbott with many things, which in essence boiled down to misusing government property.[24] There is nothing in the record showing if Outcall's charges were ever investigated, or if they were what prompted the recall of Abbott. In any case, on September 24, 1878, Leverett M. Kelly was named Indian agent at Los Pinos, replacing Abbott. Kelly was serving as Indian agent in Dakota when the need arose to find a successor to Abbott.[25] In October, Abbott asked that his replacement come as soon as possible, as certain tasks had to be completed before cold weather set in.[26] Three weeks later, Abbott wrote that he was physically unable to perform his duties, and again urged early arrival of his successor.[27] Abbott finally departed in mid-December, 1878, when he wrote the Office of Indian Affairs that his future address would be New Hampshire.[28] Abbott, like Wheeler and Bond before him, left to his successor the problem of the squatters on Indian land in Uncompahgre Park.

The Utes had told Colonel Hatch that they would be willing to discuss Uncompahgre Park further, in Washington. So soon after taking charge, agent Kelly escorted a group of Los Pinos chiefs and headmen to Washington for further talks on the Park. Kelly telegraphed the Commissioner of Indian Affairs from St. Louis just before the end of 1878 that the Ute delegation would soon be in Washington.[29] Presumably to help move the negotiations along, Interior Secretary Interior Secretary Schurz authorized the expenditure in Washington of $100 to buy sundry articles of clothing for the chiefs visiting Washington,[30] and later also approved Kelly's outlay of money to repair the guns of the visiting chiefs on their return from Washington.[31] In Washington, the Utes finally agreed that for $10,000, they would give up the four mile square Uncompahgre Park tract with its hot spring.[32]

On return to Colorado, Agent Kelly reported to Washington that the Utes who had visited there seemed pleased at their treatment.[33] In March, Kelly con-

24. Letter Outcall to Interior Secretary Schurz, July 19, 1878, NARA M234, Roll 209.
25. Letter Acting CIA to the Secretary of Interior, Sept. 23, 1878, NARA M808, Roll 13.
26. Letter Abbott to the CIA, Oct. 22,1878, NARA M234, Roll 208.
27. Letter Abbott to the CIA, Nov. 12,1878, NARA M234, Roll 208.
28. Letter Abbott to the CIA, Dec. 18,1878, NARA M234, Roll 208.
29. Telegram Kelly to the CIA, Dec. 29, 1878, NARA M234, Roll 210.
30. Letter Interior Secretary Schurz to the CIA, Jan. 16, 1879, NARA M234, Roll 209.
31. Secretary Schurz to the CIA, March 22, 1879, NARA M234, Roll 209.
32. CIA, 1878, Page XXXVIII.

firmed to Washington that the Utes were indeed willing to sell the four mile
square strip encompassing Uncompahgre Park for $10,000, and added that they
wanted to have mineral surveyor Charles Wheeler of Ouray town make the necessary survey as soon as possible.[34] A written agreement was prepared for the
Commissioner of Indian Affairs, which the requisite 3/4 of males of the Tabeguache, Yampa, Grand River, and Uintah bands[35] would sign at the Los Pinos
agency. There, Ouray was the first Indian to sign. The signatures of the Indians
at Los Pinos were witnessed by agent Kelly, and the chief herder on April 12,
1879.[36] A copy of the signed agreement for the sale of Uncompahgre Park was
sent to the White House at the end of April.[37] Soon Kelley was asking Washington when the Indians would get their $10,000, as the Indians were becoming
insistent.[38] Kelly's tenure as Indian agent at Los Pinos was short; he resigned not
long after his return to Colorado from Washington, the resignation to take effect
upon qualification of a successor.[39] Although the Ute's sale of Uncompahgre
Park did not confer land titles upon the squatters, the agreement to sell ended the
efforts of the Los Pinos agents to get help from the military to oust the squatters
from that tract. White encroachment elsewhere on the reservation was still a
problem, as we will see. But the focus of attention shifted soon away from Los
Pinos, to the White River Agency.

Kelly's successor as agent at Los Pinos was Wilson M. Stanley, connected with
a small newspaper in Moultrie County, Illinois, chosen in March, 1879.[40] Stanley had some problem in obtaining sureties to endorse his required $10,000
bond.[41] He received an advance of travel money and departed Illinois at the end
of June, 1879.[42] His time at Los Pinos also would be brief. When Stanley reached
Los Pinos on July 5, 1879,[43] Kelly had already departed. It was chief herder William H. Berry who officially turned over the agency keys to Stanley on July 6.[44]

---

33. Letter Kelly to the CIA, February 8, 1879, NARA M234, Roll 210.
34. Letter Kelly to the CIA, March 8, 1879, NARA M234, Roll 210.
35. The Muache, Capote and Wiminuche had already given up their claim.
36. Agreement of April 12, 1879, NARA M234, Roll 210.
37. Letter Interior Secretary Schurz to the CIA, May 1, 1879, NARA M234, Roll 209.
38. Telegram Kelly to the CIA, April 20, 1879, NARA M234, Roll 210.
39. Letter Interior Secretary Schurz to Kelly, March 22, 1879, NARA M234, Roll 209.
40. Letter Stanley to the CIA, March 22, 1879, NARA M234, Roll 211.
41. Stanley completed his bond formalities before a Clerk of Court in Sullivan, Illinois,
    June 20, 1879, NARA M234, Roll 211.
42. Letter Stanley to the CIA, June 28, 1879, NARA M234, Roll 211.
43. Letter Stanley to the CIA, July 6, 1879, NARA M234, Roll 212.
44. Letter Stanley to the CIA, August 1, 1879, NARA M234, Roll 212.

As most new agents do, Stanley reported to Washington finding conditions bad at the agency. He called the past attempts at agriculture a failure, and asked for permission to buy hay and grain for the agency stock. More optimistically, Stanley told Washington in September that many of his Indians were talking of trying next season to raise some food for themselves. He said they should indeed do that, as he thought they had been half starved by agents in the past.[45]

---

45.   Letter Stanley to the CIA, September 1, 1879, NARA M234, Roll 212.

5

The Meeker Revolt, Ouray Dies

But now the White River agency, not Los Pinos, became the focus of Indian affairs in Colorado. On July 5, 1879, the Surveyor General of Colorado telegraphed his superior in Washington alleging that Ute Indians were preventing his field men from doing their work.[1] Also on July 5, Colorado Governor Pitkin telegraphed the Commissioner of Indian Affairs alleging that White River Utes were going off the reservation and destroying forests and game near the North and Middle Parks of Colorado. Pitkin called this an organized Indian effort to destroy the timber of Colorado. He urged that the "savages" be removed to Indian Territory, from where they could no longer destroy "the finest forests in this state."[2] The Commandant of the Army Post at Fort Steele, Wyoming, the same Major Thornburg who would later lose his life in a Ute ambush, investigated the reports of rampaging Utes in northern Colorado, and reported to his superiors that apart from killing game, the Utes had committed no depredations.[3]

Were Colorado officials simply trying to pressure Washington to remove all the Utes from the state? There is little doubt that most Coloradans wanted the Utes out,[4] but Washington must bear some of the blame for the problems which arose at the White River agency. Interior Secretary Schurz had chosen a friend, Nathan S. Meeker, to be agent there. Meeker seemed to lack the proper qualifications for the job. In naming Meeker, Schurz bypassed the understanding that the Unitarian Church would nominate persons to be Indian agents in Colorado.[5]

---

1. Letter Commissioner of the General Land Office to the Secretary of Interior, July 8, 1879, NARA M234, Roll 210.
2. CIA, 1879, pp. *XVIII to* XXXVIII.
3. Report of Brigadier General George C. Crook, Commanding the Department of the Platte, August 4, 1879, NARA M234, Roll 212.
4. Letter Wheeler to the CIA, October 29, 1877, CIA, 1877, p. 43.
5. Edward E. Hill, *The Office of Indian Affairs, 1824-1880: Historical Sketches*, Clearwater Publishing Co., New York, N. Y., 1874, p. 49.

Schurz did go through the motions of trying to get the Unitarians to nominate Meeker, but they said he was totally unknown to them.[6] Provoked or not by Agent Meeker, some of the Indians at the White River agency rebelled in October, 1879, killing Meeker and taking 3 women as hostages.

Earlier, the Indians also ambushed an Army unit under Major Thornburg sent from Fort Steele to investigate Meeker's reports of trouble at the White River agency, killing Thornburg and 12 others in the so-called Battle of Milk River. The White River difficulties at first drew little attention, with the *New York Times* of September 16, 1879 devoting less than 2 column inches to a vague report of trouble. By October 3, the Ute uprising and the ambush of the Thornburg party was the lead item on page one of the *Times*. Various persons quoted in the lengthy article of that day presumed that Meeker was dead since he had not been heard from for over a week. The article contained much speculation as to what triggered the revolt, but made clear that none of the Utes at Los Pinos, except possibly Chief Sapavanaro, was involved. From New York, Commissioner of Indian Affairs Hayt telegraphed his deputy in Washington saying that the proximate cause of the uprising was the attempt of Colorado Governor Pitkin and his authorities to enforce civil process on the Ute reservation, contrary to treaty provisions.[7] On December 8, 1897, when the worst of the White River crisis had passed, the Senate adopted a resolution calling for the Interior Department to give it copies of all messages concerning the matter. Interior Secretary Schurz responded on January 5, 1880—thanks to which historians now have an extensive record of the so-called Meeker Revolt, and a printed one no less.[8] While the records turned over by Schurz focus on events at the White River Agency, they also show the important pacifying role played by Ouray and others at the Los Pinos agency.

Interior Secretary Schurz, in Colorado at the time trouble started, met with Governor Pitkin. Pitkin suggested to Schurz that former Tabeguache Agent Charles Adams might be able to head off a developing battle between the White River Utes and the troops advancing from Fort Steele. Adams told them he would be willing to try, provided his Post Office employer ordered him to do so. Schurz quickly prevailed upon the Post Office Department to detail Adams temporarily to the Indian Service.[9] Schurz in turn asked Pitkin to ensure that the

6.   Letter American Unitarian Association to Schurz, March 7,1878, NARA M234, Roll 209.
7.   Telegram Hayt to the Acting CIA, Oct. 3, 1879, NARA M234, Roll 209.
8.   Letter Schurz to the President of the Senate, Senate Executive Document No. 31 (46-2), Serial Set 1882.

Colorado militia and armed citizens confined themselves to protecting life and property only outside the Ute reservation.[10] Asked to help, Ouray said he was willing to try. He indicated that he had influence with the White River Utes and thought he could help settle the matter. Through the Postmaster at Lake City and Governor Pitkin, Ouray in turn requested that Agent Stanley be removed at once.[11]

Before arriving at Los Pinos, Adams asked several things from Schurz. One was the assignment to Los Pinos of another former Los Pinos agent, one-time Lieutenant Governor of Colorado Lafayette Head, who understood the Ute language.[12] Another was authority to employ 30 Indian scouts. A third was the quiet movement of troops from Fort Garland to Lake City, where they would be only 50 miles from the Agency.[13] Schurz came through on the first two. After consulting on the third with General P. H. Sheridan, commanding the Army's Department of the Missouri within whose purview Fort Garland fell, the idea of moving troops to Lake City was rejected. Schurz and Sheridan thought that move might undercut Ouray's efforts.[14]

After consulting with Ouray at Los Pinos, Adams went to meet with the White River rebels. The rebels had fled south of the Colorado River to put distance between themselves and the troops advancing from Fort Steele. Adams took with him two or three white men[15] and some Indian chiefs. Adams reached the rebel's small camp on the morning of October 21, 1879. The women kidnaped at the White River agency were scattered about the rebel camp, but unharmed. After considerable talking, with the Indians wanting to hold the hostages until the troops were stopped, Adams got them to release the captives first. Adams then went to head off the advance of the military,[16] while the hostages were escorted to Los Pinos by others in the Adams party.

---

9.   Adams told the story of his involvement in settling the White River problem before a House investigating committee. See House Miscellaneous Document 38 (46-2), Serial Set 1931.

10.   Telegram Secretary Schurz to Governor Pitkin, October 13, 1879, *op. cit.*

11.   Telegram Governor Pitkin to the Secretary of the Interior Schurz, October 12, 1879, CIA, 1879, pp. XVIII to XXXVIII.

12.   Head died in Denver in 1897.

13.   Telegram Adams to Secretary Schurz, Nov. 2, 1879, *op. cit.*

14.   Telegram Secretary Schurz to Adams, Nov. 5, 1879, *op.* cit.

15.   One of the whites was Count Doenhof, Secretary of the German Legation in Washington, who had met Adams on the train and asked to be included. See House Miscellaneous Document 38, Serial Set 1931.

16.   *Ibid.*

Getting the hostages released was not the end of the matter; the guilty had to be punished. Adams got back to Los Pinos on November 9, and went to Ouray's house to meet about 20 of the chiefs and head men of the White River Utes who had come in response to Ouray's orders.[17] The purpose of the gathering was to take testimony from the Indians involved in the uprising, in order to determine who should be held accountable. It was then that Ouray was at his best, swearing in the witnesses in Ute fashion, acting partly as prosecutor and partly as defense attorney. He also showed an understanding for the white man's concept of justice, asserting at these hearings a Fifth Amendment right for accused Utes: no one should be forced to give testimony that might incriminate himself. On December 6, 1879, the White River representatives finally agreed to surrender the culpable parties to face court proceedings, but not in Colorado.[18] They did not think they could get a fair trial there. Ouray left Los Pinos to go with the White River chiefs to assist in bringing in those guilty of slaying Meeker and ambushing the troops.

Adams returned to Denver and Colonel Edward Hatch took over at Los Pinos. Hatch reported to Washington that it was certain that the culpable Indians would be surrendered, "as certain as any arrangements with the Indians" could be.[19] But when White River chiefs Jack, Colorow and Sawawick returned to Los Pinos on December 21, they did not bring all the prisoners expected. Hatch told Washington he thought the missing had either escaped, or that the three chiefs lacked the power to turn them over.[20]

Whether Los Pinos agent Stanley played any significant role in these events is not evident. Stanley did relay to Southern Ute agent Henry Page Ouray's appreciation of the Southern Ute decision not to get involved with the uprising at the White River agency.[21] Stanley, not Adams, also was the person to whom Schurz gave permission for hiring the Indian scouts.[22] But after the White River revolt was settled, Interior Secretary Schurz on December 26 accepted Stanley's "resignation," to take effect December 31, 1879.[23] Stanley's departure being unplanned, no replacement was on tap. So agency clerk George Sherman on Jan-

17. Telegram Adams to Secretary Schurz, Nov. 10, 1879, Senate Executive Document No. 31, (46-2), serial set 1882.
18. Telegram Hatch to Secretary Schurz, Dec. 6, 1879, *op. cit.*.
19. Telegram Hatch to Secretary Schurz, Dec. 13, 1879, *op. cit.*
20. Hatch telegram to Secretary Schurz, December 21, 1897, op. cit.
21. Letter Stanley to Page, (Oct. 1879?), NARA M234, Roll 211.
22. Letter Secretary Schurz to the CIA, Nov. 3, 1879, NARA M234, Roll 209.
23. Letter Secretary Schurz to Stanley, Dec. 26, 1879, *op. cit.*

uary 1, 1880 became acting agent at Los Pinos until a more permanent replacement could be found.

Early in January, 1880, a delegation of chiefs led by Ouray but including representatives of the White Rivers and the Southern Utes in addition to the Tabeguache set out for Washington to negotiate further limits on Ute land holdings in Colorado. The Utes' trip did not begin well. A Colorado-based *New York Times* correspondent reported in the issue of January 8, 1880 from Pueblo: "Twelve Ute Indians in charge of Lt. Taylor of the 9th cavalry, with 10 men, arrived here today, and immediately proceeded east on the Santa Fe. They had ordered dinner at the union depot hotel, but the sight of a large crowd of pale faces destroyed their appetite. They at once boarded the train and left without eating. Between 2,000 and 3,000 people had congregated at the depot to see the savages. 'Hang the red Devils,' 'Shoot the murdering thieves,' and like expressions were heard from crowd. The Indians were bombarded by coal thrown by boys who had boarded a coal train on an adjoining track."[24] The Indian-unfriendly tone of the article reflected public attitudes in Colorado, not the attitude of the New York paper as later editorials made clear.[25] W. H. Berry was with the Ute delegation in the capacity of interpreter. He had been chief herder at Los Pinos under Agent Kelley, and had been left in temporary charge of the agency when Kelley departed prior to the arrival of Stanley, his successor.

When the delegation arrived in Washington, the people who gathered to see the famous Ouray outside the Tremont House in Washington were curious, not hostile like those in Pueblo. Secretary Schurz delayed the talks awaiting the arrival of Charles Adams.[26] Adams was slow in arriving as he had been delegated to escort to Fort Leavenworth the Utes surrendered as being culpable in the Meeker Massacre. Interior asked the War Department, and the latter agreed, to furnish a military escort across Colorado for the Adams party. Fort Leavenworth initially was uncomfortable about accepting Indian prisoners for an indefinite period, but was instructed from Washington to take in any and all Indians that Adams might want to turn over.[27]

The Washington talks with the Utes on giving up their reservation dragged on. Only in mid-March could Schurz report to Congress that an agreement had been worked out. He submitted to the Indian Affairs committees of both houses

24. *New York Times*, January 8, 1880, page one, column two
25. *New York Times*, January 12, 1880, page one, column three.
26. *New York Times*, January 12, 1880, page one, column three.
27. Telegram General Sherman to General Pope, Feb. 25, 1880, NARA M234, Roll 214.

the text of a bill to implement the agreement reached.[28] The Ute chiefs agreed to surrender the guilty parties for trial and pledged to use their best efforts to get their people to cede their present reservation in Colorado, except for lands along the New Mexico border reserved for the Southern Utes, and lands near the junction of the Colorado and Gunnison Rivers intended for the Tabeguache. The chiefs agreed not to interfere with travel on highways lawfully opened through the retained lands. In return, the chiefs insisted that the lands their people would receive be properly surveyed and formal title conveyed, which lands would not be subject to alienation and would be exempt from taxation for 25 years. Furthermore, the $60,000 in past annuities due them should be paid in cash as soon as the Indians ratified that agreement. This money to go ½ to the Tabeguache or Uncompahgre Utes, 1/3 to the Southern Utes, and 1/6 to the White River Utes. Further, the United States would pay the Utes $50,000 a year, stipulated as consideration for their relinquishment of the 1868 Ute reservation. The annuity of $25,000 a year set in the 1868 treaty would also continue.[29] The $50,000 annuity promised in the March, 1880 agreement represented interest at the going rate of 4 percent on the amount of $1,250,000. Since the Ute reservation contained over 10 million acres, the tribe was being paid about 12 cents per acre. Far less than the minimum $1.25 cash per acre set in the act opening the Ute reservation as the minimum price to be paid by whites buying reservation land from Uncle Sam's General Land Office. One bright spot for the Indians in the law of June 15, 1880 approving the March agreement was that Ouray's beloved hot spring, with the surrounding "4 mile tract" which the Utes had clung to so tenaciously, would not be put into the public domain for squatters to claim for themselves. Instead, Section 8 of the act set the spring apart "for the enjoyment of the people," including Ute Indians, under a regime like that earlier set up for Yellowstone Park.[30] This provision was repealed just 4 years later.[31]

Back at the Los Pinos agency, acting agent Sherman like his predecessors had to deal with problems in agency relations with the citizens of Ouray. He reported to Washington receiving, shortly after he was placed in charge, an anonymous letter about white encroachment on the reservation. He also sent a copy of the notice he proposed publishing in Ouray newspapers in reply.[32] Sherman also had

---

28.   *New York Times*, March 13, 1880, page 5, column four.
29.   The agreement is reproduced in 21 Stat. 199 *et. seq.*, the Act of June 15, 1880 which amended and provided for implementation of the March agreement.
30.   21 Stat. 194.
31.   23 Stat. 22
32.   Letter Sherman to the CIA, Jan. 8, 1880, NARA M234, Roll 213.

to handle a complaint from the trustees of Ouray town about Indians coming into town in search of whiskey or ammunition. The trustees asked Sherman to keep the Indians out of the town, and said they would do their best to keep Ouray residents off the reservation.[33] Sherman sent a new complaint to Washington in March about white encroachment on the reservation. Interior Secretary Schurz thought this report alarming enough to bring to the attention of the Cabinet on March 16. It was decided that Ouray and his associates should return quickly to Los Pinos, and try to prevent the Utes from ousting the intruders by force of arms. Simultaneously, Schurz issued a public notice that the Ute reservation was not yet part of the public domain, and that the Interior Department would not recognize any claims of mineral location made there before the reservation had been officially proclaimed part of the public domain.[34] This notice was not uniformly observed.

When the Ute negotiators left Washington for Colorado, Schurz wrote the Secretary of War asking that an Army detachment meet them and escort them from the railhead at Alamosa to Los Pinos. Schurz also suggested that troops be stationed around Los Pinos "in readiness."[35] The Secretary of War replied that troops from Fort Garland would escort the delegation only as far as the Cochetopa Pass,[36] but did send instructions to the Chicago Headquarters of the Department of the Missouri to be ready to move troops from Fort Garland to Los Pinos later in the year when supply wagons could reach the Agency.[37]

The Commandant at Fort Garland, Colonel R. S. McKenzie, did what a good military man would do: he sent a scout to the Los Pinos region to report back to him what the troops would have to face later in the year. The scout was a civilian, Christopher Gilson, who sent back a series of illuminating letters to Fort Garland. In late April, Gilson reported that for some unknown reason, Chief Ouray was depressed and unwilling to talk to anyone.[38] In mid-May, Gilson reported to McKenzie on a horse racing meet held at Ouray's farm, attended by some 500 Indians including some from both the Southern and White River agencies. These letters made clear that Gilson had become friends with a Mexican houseman

---

33. Letter trustees of the town of Ouray to Sherman, Jan. 14, 1880, NARA M234, Roll 213.
34. *New York Times*, March 17, 1880, page one, column four
35. Letter Schurz to the Secretary of War, March 26, 1880, NARA M234, Roll 214.
36. Letter the Secretary of War to Schurz, March 27, 1880, NARA M234, Roll 214.
37. Letter General Sherman, Washington, to General Whipple, Department of the Missouri, Chicago, March 27, 1880, NARA M234, Roll 214.
38. Letter Gilson to McKenzie, April 23, 1880, NARA M234, Roll 214.

working for Ouray. Gilson also refers to a "boy," apparently an Indian boy, who helped him carry out observations of the Indians without arousing suspicion.[39] McKenzie later left Ft. Garland, reported to his headquarters at the end of May that he had arrived at Los Pinos with a cavalry detachment, and that the complete party, with supply wagons, was expected on June 2.[40]

This was the start of a military post officially called the Cantonment on the Uncompahgre, but less formally Fort Crawford. Some of the letters sent by the Commanding Officer there to his superiors reporting on talks with Los Pinos Indian agent Berry provide valuable insight into the events in the 15 months before the Los Pinos Agency was closed.[41]

Site of Old Fort Crawford

39.   Letters Gilson to McKenzie, May 15 and 17, 1880, NARA M234, Roll 214.
40.   Letter McKenzie to the Assistant Adjutant General, Department of the Missouri, May 31, 1880, NARA M234, Roll 214.
41.   NARA Record Group 393, Part 5, Entry 2, Volume 1, Letters Sent from Fort Crawford, Colorado, Oct. 1, 1880 to Jan. 3, 1882. Hereafter referred to simply as Crawford.

In one sense, the Utes at Los Pinos profited from the arrival of the troops. Soon after he became acting agent in January on the recall of agent Stanley, Sherman had allowed former agent W. D. Wheeler to open trading operations at the Los Pinos agency. Sherman reported the Los Pinos agency had firm orders from Washington to keep the Indians out of the town of Ouray, yet the Indians wanted supplies of such things as coffee and sugar which could be bought in the town. At first, Sherman allowed the Indians to leave orders at his office, which with the necessary money were carried by the stage driver to the town of Ouray to be filled. But some Indians had no money, and wanted instead to send goods such as buckskins to be traded. This was hardly workable. Wheeler, who had moved to the town of Ouray on being discharged as agent, happened to be at Los Pinos at the time as a guest of former agent Stanley. Wheeler had suggested that he could pick up supplies of coffee and sugar at Lake City or in the town of Ouray to sell to the Indians, if Sherman would allow him to use the old trader's store. This seemed like a sensible arrangement, meeting the needs of the Utes while keeping them out of the town of Ouray. Soon after Chief Ouray returned from Washington, Sherman ascertained that Wheeler had sold Ouray powder and lead. Selling ammunition to Indians was strictly forbidden. Wheeler attempted to justify these actions, saying that Ouray was a privileged Indian and entitled to buy ammunition. Still, Sherman put an end to Wheeler's trading activities at Los Pinos.[42] After Colonel McKenzie's troops arrived, Sherman informed Washington that he had given verbal permission to the military sutler to sell coffee and sugar to the Indians at the Los Pinos agency. He did this at the urgent request of the Utes, and with Ouray's approval. He noted that the arrangement prevented the Utes from going into town, and saved his office much trouble.[43]

Wheeler did not stay long in Colorado after Sherman stopped his trading activities. A few months later, Wheeler wrote the Indian Department from Washington, D. C., on stationary of the United States Engineer Office, Geographical Survey West of the 100th Meridian, asking that the Indian Department pay for his return to his home in Massachusetts.[44]

When W. H. Berry reported to Los Pinos as agent early in July, 1880, Sherman reverted to his regular status as agency clerk. Sherman then asked for and was granted two months' leave.[45] When Sherman failed to return on the agreed

42.   Letter Sherman to the CIA, May 18, 1880, NARA M234, Roll 214.
43.   Letter Sherman to the CIA, June 3, 1880, NARA M234, Roll 214.
44.   Letter Wheeler to the CIA, June 16, 1880, NARA M234, Roll 214.
45.   Letter Sherman to the CIA, June 4, 1880, NARA M234, Roll 214.

date, Berry abruptly discharged him as clerk. Sherman was much aggrieved and protested, but to no avail. He had, after all, done what seems to have been a good job as acting agent.

It fell to Berry to submit to Washington the Los Pinos contribution to the 1880 Annual Report of the Commissioner of Indian Affairs. Berry said that the Indians belonging to his agency were the Tabeguache, numbering in all 1,500 souls. There was not one mixed or half breed among the band, he claimed. He wrote that the Los Pinos agency was just 25 miles from Ouray town, but 210 miles from the nearest railway station at Alamosa. It was 80 miles from the nearest telegraph station, then at Lake City. The agency buildings are all in fair condition, he said, a contrast from the usual complaints of a new agent. He noted that a trader had put up one building at the agency at his own expense, and that Messrs. Sanderson and Co., of the Overland Mail and Stage route, had put up a frame building for use as a way station and accommodation for part of their stock. Some 30 Indians were farming, including chiefs, headmen and others, cultivating in aggregate 75 acres. Berry estimated that they might raise this year 1,500 bushels of potatoes, 500 bushels of corn, 25 bushels of wheat, 75 bushels of oats, 200 bushels of turnips, as well as some onions, squash, melons, cabbage and pumpkins. Part of this the Indians would sell to United States troops in this vicinity, and part to whites passing through, receiving good prices. The balance would be consumed by themselves at home. A few of the Indians, he wrote, had proved to be very successful raising herds of horses and sheep. Some ten or twelve families had then 150 head of good stock cattle. During the year, 160 rods of fencing had been put up by the Indians. Berry said that the agency had its own farm of one acre along the river bottom land, where agency employees cultivated a small quantity of green corn, potatoes, cucumbers and squash. This was not as much as hoped because the press of agency business required the constant attention of all employees. There was but one house occupied Indians, the one built for Chief Ouray. Other Indians reportedly were anxious to have good log houses built, and would willingly assist in putting them up.[46] All in all, Berry seemed upbeat in describing the Los Pinos agency. In reality, its days were numbered.

On June 15, 1880, the President signed a law[47] amending and implementing the March 3, 1880 agreement with the Utes on the sale of their reservation in Colorado. The major changes required by Congress were to ban any payments to the White River Utes so long as any guilty parties in the Meeker Massacre were at

---

46.   Letter Berry to the CIA, September 1, 1880, CIA, 1880, p. 14.
47.   21 Stat. 199.

liberty in U.S. territory, and to use some funds otherwise due the White River Utes to pay compensation to the victims of that event. Congress also inserted a provision asking the President to divert up to $10,000 from monies due all the Utes to pay the expenses of educating Ute youths away from the reservation. Here Congress had in mind the just opened Indian School at the Army Barracks in Carlisle, Pennsylvania. That school, founded by an Army officer with the strong encouragement of Interior Secretary Schurz, had received its first students in October, 1879, from the Sioux Agencies in South Dakota.[48] Sheldon Jackson, overseeing the Presbyterian-run Indian agencies in New Mexico, Arizona and elsewhere, wrote to the Commissioner of Indian Affairs to urge that the Ute Commission in its talks with the Utes solicit Ute agreement to send children to Carlisle.[49] This would be quite a stretch; very few Indian children had attended the schools agents had run at various times at the Los Pinos agency. But some Ute children eventually did go to Carlisle.

The June 15, 1880 law approving the agreement on sale of the Ute reservation called for appointment of a five member Ute Commission to obtain the required signatures of 3/4 of adult males to the agreement, with a clerk to handle the paper work. George W. Manypenny, one time editor of a newspaper in Columbus, Ohio and long time advocate of fair treatment of Indians, was named Commission Chairman. Three other members were Easterners who had held the rank of colonel in the Union forces in the Civil War. The fifth member, Otto Mears, was quite familiar with the Utes from having held many contracts to deliver supplies to the Los Pinos agency. At the time he served on the Commission, his company was annoying the Utes by running a large herd of cattle along the Uncompahgre River on land used by the Indians for their own stock.[50] In 1881 before the Utes were removed from Los Pinos, a company controlled by Mears began building a toll road from the Los Pinos agency to Fort Lewis near the Southern Ute reservation, a distance of 125 miles.[51]

The Ute Commission going to the three Ute agencies had a manifold assignment. Their main task of course was to obtain the signatures of 3/4 of the adult males at each agency accepting the agreement as modified. The principal modifi-

---

48. Richard Henry Pratt, *Battlefield and Classroom, Four Decades with the American Indian, 1867-1904*, New Haven, Yale University Press, 1964, pp. 212-229.

49. Letter Jackson to the CIA, June 17, 1880, NARA M234, Roll 213.

50. Letter Major J. H. Fletcher to the Assistant Adjutant General, Department of the Missouri, Nov. 13, 1880, NARA M234, Roll 214.

51. Letter Commandant at Fort Crawford to the Assistant Adjutant General, Department of the Missouri, May 30, 1881, Crawford, p. 154.

cations took away certain sums originally allotted the White River Utes, which sums would instead be paid to those who had suffered at the hands of the White Rivers. The principle of using Indian annuity money to pay compensation for damages caused by Indians had been established in the 1868 treaty with the Utes, but still Congress was forcing a change adverse to the Indians in a bargain struck just 3 months earlier. The Commission was also expected to ensure that the Utes cooperated in turning over for trial any remaining guilty parties from the Meeker Massacre. And the Commission was to take a census of the Utes at each agency, listing the name of the male head of each household. The Commission further was to oversee the survey of the lands to be given to the Utes in severalty, and arrange for the transfer of the Utes of these lands. Quite a lot on the Commission's plate when they came to Los Pinos.

The Manypenny Commission reached Los Pinos in early July and asked Chief Ouray to meet with them on July 16 to advise on the proprieties when the first council with the Utes was to be held. The Commissioners subsequently met in council on July 20, 22, 23, 26 and 28 with both the White Rivers and the Uncompahgre present. Only on that last day were some Utes finally prepared to put their marks on the agreement. Additional signatures were obtained on the 29th, 30th, and 31st of July, 1880. Under the agreement signed at Los Pinos, the Utes gave up their claims to reservation lands, except for those along the La Plata River where the Southern Utes were already settled, and those on the Grand River near the mouth of the Gunnison River, to which the Tabeguache were to move.[52] The White River Utes agreed to leave Colorado altogether, and go to the Uintah Reservation in Utah. That accomplished, members of the Ute Commission left Los Pinos in early August with a military escort for the Southern Ute Agency to obtain the necessary signatures there. The Commission invited Ouray and other Uncompahgre head men to go as well, to assist them in getting signatures from the Southern Utes.[53]

In an August 26th telegram to Washington, Commission head Manypenny reported his presentation of the agreement to the Southern Utes at their agency at Ignacio, and added that Ouray was present, but quite sick.[54] If Ouray lived in many ways like a white man, at Ignacio on August 24, 1880, he died like a true Indian. His final hours were attended by an Indian medicine man so continu-

---

52. Agreement in Senate Executive Document 31 (46-2), Serial Set 1943.

53. Report of Ute Commission, January 20, 1881, Senate Executive Document 31 (46-3), serial set 1943

54. Telegram Manypenney to the Secretary of Interior, August 26, 1880, NARA M234, Roll 214. Telegram delayed in transmission.

ously that the white doctors were able to get in to see him only long enough to determine they could do nothing for him. When Ouray died, his body was wrapped in a blanket, thrown over a horse, and taken away by a few companions. No one else was permitted to accompany the burial party.[55] Ouray's body was buried in some rocks about 2 miles south of the Southern Ute agency. In keeping with Ute custom, three horses belonging to Ouray and his saddle were destroyed at the spot to accompany him to the Happy Hunting Ground.[56]

55. Mrs. C. W. Weigle, "The Death of Ouray, Chief of the Utes," _Colorado Magazine,_ Vol. 7, p, 190.
56. Florence E. Whittier, "The Grave of Chief Ouray," _Colorado Magazine_, Volume I, p. 316.

Ouray Death Site, Ignacio, CO

On August 31, a runner arrived at Ignacio from the Los Pinos Agency with a message from Meacham, the Ute Commission member left behind at Los Pinos, that the Tabeguache wanted Ouray's remains shipped there in a zinc casket with a glass face for interment. After some initial objections, the Southern Utes said they would go along with the wishes of those at Los Pinos. Some members of the Ute Commission then went to inspect Ouray's burial site, but decided that due to the decomposition of unembalmed body, such a transfer could not be effected until the arrival of cold weather.[57] Ouray's remains stayed where first buried until they were re-interred, with appropriate ceremony, on May 25, 1924 at the Southern Ute Agency cemetery at Ignacio.[58]

Ouray's death brought out a Ute custom of destroying the belongings of a dead Indian male. Berry informed Washington that only by great effort had he dissuaded Ouray's widow, Chipeta, from burning down the fine house that Ouray had built.[59] Subsequently, Chipeta firmly refused to allow that house to be used as distribution point for money being paid to those Utes who signed the agreement for the sale of their reservation.[60] The Los Pinos Utes chose Saponavaro as Ouray's successor,[61] something that Berry welcomed (and indeed had worked for).[62] But Saponavaro lacked Ouray's great ability to influence others.[63]

By September 11, well within the four months' period specified in the law, Manypenny's Ute Commission had secured the assent to the agreement of the required 3/4 of the adult males of the Ute bands. This ratification by the Utes was submitted to the Secretary of the Treasury by the Secretary of Interior on September 24, for steps to be initiated to make the funds due the Indians available for disbursement,[64] except to the White River band who were supposed first to hand over for trial any of the band guilty of participating in the Meeker Revolt. Although the Commission had not taken custody of some still free but presumed guilty White River Utes, the members of the Commission, less Colonel Meacham who had stayed at Los Pinos, sent to Interior Secretary Schurz from Denver on October 15 a certificate stating that they had tried diligently to apprehend the missing presumed guilty parties, that the Utes had in no way impeded their efforts, and that the Commission believed that any remaining guilty parties not already in custody were either dead or had fled outside the limits of the United States. The Commission urged that they be authorized to begin paying the White River Utes the sums due them.[65]

---

57. Letter Manypenny to Schurz, September 20, 1880, SenExecDoc 31 (46-3), pp. 19-20.

58. Weigle, *op. cit.*, p. 191.

59. Letter Berry to the CIA, September 1,1880, CIA 1880, p. 14.

60. Telegram Townsend to the CIA, Nov. 28, 1880, NARA M234, roll 214.

61. *New York Times*, Sept. 1, 1880, page 1 col. 7.

62. Letter Berry to the CIA, September 1,1880, CIA 1880, p. 14.

63. Letter Commandant at Fort Crawford to the Assistant Adjutant General, Department of the Missouri, April 14, 1881, Crawford, p. 114.

64. CIA, 1880, pp. XXIV and XXV.

65. Sen. Exec. Doc. 31 (46-3), p. 29, Serial Set 1943.

Meacham six days earlier from Los Pinos had advised the Secretary of Interior that "the murderers of Meeker have been expelled from the White River band, and that they were now somewhere in the north or northwest."[66] On October 25, the Acting Secretary of Interior informed Commission Chairman Manypenny that the President had accepted their judgement on the still missing Indians and authorized the Commission to begin making payment including to the White Rivers.[67] However, on November 16, 1880, Secretary Schurz instructed Meacham that payments should not be made to any White Rivers at Los Pinos, but only at their new home on the Uintah Reservation in Utah.[68]

Before the funds were paid out and the lands surveyed for a new home for the Tabeguache along the Grand River, an unexpected problem arose which for a time threatened to escalate into a new Indian war. The problem involved a conflict between Federal and state responsibility for law enforcement on an Indian reservation. Early in October, 1880, the son of Chief Shavano was killed by a white man named A. D. Jackson, with the only witnesses to the shooting being those directly involved. Colorado Governor Pitkin cabled Interior Secretary Schurz on October 15, 1880 with the version of events provided by the whites. These claimed they were freighting goods into Ouray town through the reservation when they were set upon by a group of Indians. A. D. Jackson grabbed a rifle and fired at the attacking Indians in self defense. All the Indians rode off, and the whites did not know whether any of the Indians had been hit. Only on the next day, when Agent Berry came with 15 soldiers and accompanied by 125 armed Indians, did they learn that one of the Indians had been killed. Berry arrested the shooter, A. D. Jackson, in accordance with Article 6 of the 1868 treaty. This article provided that any person subject to the authority of the United States who commits a crime against the person or property of an Indian shall be arrested by U.S. authorities and tried "under the laws of the United States." So Jackson would be tried in a court, this instance in Gunnison. Berry turned Jackson over to three State of Colorado officials who were to take him to Gunnison. Agent Berry reportedly prevented any soldiers from escorting the arresting posse back to Gunnison.[69]

Before this posse had gone 5 miles, they were ambushed by some Indians, who took Jackson away and subsequently killed him.[70] Colorado held that agent

---

66. Sen. Exec. Doc. 31 (46-3), p. 32.
67. Sen. Exec. Doc. 31 (46-3), p. 31
68. Sen. Exec. Doc. 31 (46-3), p. 35.
69. Telegram General Pope to General Sheridan, Oct. 12, 1880, NARA M234, Roll 214.

Berry, by denying a military escort, was culpable in Jackson's death, and sent State officials to Los Pinos to arrest him, along with those Indians involved. This created a real jurisdictional conflict. Article 6 of the 1868 treaty called for the Indians to detain Jackson's murderers and turn them over to United States' authorities. The Indians claimed ignorance of who was responsible, and certainly were not about to detain agent Berry who had their trust. Could state officials come onto an Indian reservation to execute a state warrant for the arrest of an Indian Service officer? Would the United States protect its agent, against the howls of Colorado citizens for rough justice? Berry at first thought that he was beyond the jurisdiction of the Colorado courts, and asked the Commandant at Fort Crawford for protection.[71] Subsequently, the Commandant reported receiving information that a mob was being organized in Ouray to invade the reservation to seize agent Berry and those Indians who had taken part in killing Jackson. He was aware that Colorado newspapers had published reports of indignation meetings held in Ouray, but did not think the Indians would allow their agent to be taken away.[72] What to do?

Governor Pitkin on October 15 asked Washington to move the Tabeguache Utes to the mouth of the Uncompahgre River, even as far away as the Grand River. He noted that some freighters were now afraid to go into Ouray town because of what had happened to the Jackson party. Pitkin said that while Colorado wanted all the Utes removed from the state, the state would not block fulfillment of the agreement reached by the Ute Commission. In particular, Pitkin did not se how the arrest of agent Berry would complicate implementation of the agreement.[73] Three days later, Commissioner Meacham cabled Washington, through the Western Union facilities now available at the Cantonment on the Uncompahgre, that every Ute lodge had been moved down river so that the Cantonment now lay between the Utes and the town of Ouray.[74]

Washington told Berry that he had to accept the arrest authority of Federal law enforcement officials if they came with a proper warrant.[75] Berry then sub-

---

70. Sen. Exec. Doc.31, p. 51.
71. Letter Commandant at Fort Crawford to the Assistant Adjutant General, Department of the Missouri, October 11, 1880, Crawford, pp. 13 to 15.
72. Telegram Commandant at Fort Crawford to the Assistant Adjutant General, Department of the Missouri, October 19, 1880, Crawford, p. 23
73. Sen. Exec. Doc. 31 (46-3), p. 52.
74. Sen. Exec. Doc. 31 (46-3), p. 30.
75. Telegram Acting Secretary of Interior to Berry, Oct. 18, 1880, NARA M234, Roll 213.

mitted to arrest by the U.S. Marshall, on the advice of the U.S. District Attorney. The Department of Interior detailed veteran Indian Department employee E. C. Townsend to Los Pinos to be acting agent while Berry was under arrest.[76] Townsend thought it best for him to get to the Los Pinos agency incognito. Either he wanted to listen to open public opinion, or possibly he feared for his own safety in view of the inflamed public opinion.

Next Commissioner Meacham was arrested on arriving in Denver in mid November, on the same charges which led to Berry's arrest. Berry was annoyed at this, feeling that after Meacham's own arrest, he could not call Meacham as an impartial witness in his own trial. Ute Commission Secretary John French, viewing all these legal actions from Denver, complained that these was hampering his efforts to complete paying off the Utes.[77] Fortunately, Meacham could wire Washington from Denver on November 23, 1880 that the cases against him and Berry were postponed until April, and that he and Berry would be granted bail. He and Berry were freed the next day to go back to Los Pinos and resume the Commission's work on settling with the Utes.[78] At the same time, Washington issued orders to the Commandant at the Cantonment on the Uncompahgre to resist by force any intrusion by armed men into the reservation.[79]

The U.S. Government had a long record for slowness in making payment to Indians, a record not enhanced by its delay in completing paying the Utes for the sale of their reservation. At first, the U.S. set the date of November 28 for the final payment to the Tabeguache at Los Pinos. When Townsend heard the final payout might be delayed beyond this, he sent a telegram of protest to Washington.[80] Finally by mid December, Commission Secretary John French completed most payments due the Utes at Los Pinos. Since some households had been away and might not return to the Agency for weeks or months, French asked Washington for permission to accept Berry's receipt for the $3,000 due those families, with Berry to pay the money out when the missing families finally showed up at Los Pinos. He said the Indians would be uneasy if the cash due the families was

76. Letter Acting Secretary of Interior to the CIA, Oct. 18, 1880, NARA M234, Roll 213.
77. Letter French to Schurz, November 22, 1880, Sen. Exec. Doc. 31 (46-3), p. 35-6.
78. Telegram Meacham to Schurz, November 23, 1880, Sen. Exec. Doc. 31 (46-3), p. 36
79. Letter Secretary of War to the Secretary of Interior, Nov. 29, 1880, NARA M234, Roll 214.
80. Telegram Townsend to the CIA, Nov. 23, 1880, NARA 234, Roll 214.

taken away from Los Pinos.[81] The Interior Secretary agreed to this idea in mid-December.[82]

Left until the year 1881 was the actual removal of the Los Pinos Utes to their still unidentified new reservation, described in the 1880 agreement as lying along the Grand River near the mouth of the Gunnison River. Pending the final movement in 1881, Secretary Schurz asked for the opinion of those at Los Pinos whether it would be prudent to remove the Tabeguache away from the town of Ouray and away from the road along which white travelers were passing to reach that town and the mining camps in the San Juan Mountains.[83] He got a mixed response. Commissioner Otto Mears agreed that leaving the Tabeguache where they were risked having the Indians squander their payment money by going into town to buy liquor, but felt that the Indians might consider any short move as the final move. Furthermore, even a short move away could cause an inflow of whites into the vacated lands. Commissioner Meacham also opposed any move until the final one. He argued that the Tabeguache had Army protection where they were, and to move them away before any final settlement would invite a land rush by whites. Agent Berry on the other hand favored the immediate removal of the Tabeguache, but not for the proposed distance of just 50 miles. He thought any move should get the Tabeguache as close as possible to their final destination.[84] In the end, Interior Secretary Schurz decided that the Tabeguache should remain where they were, within easy reach of the Cantonment on the Uncompahgre for their own protection and for the maintenance of order, until the final movement in 1881.[85]

Around the end of 1880, someone in the Department of Interior wrote a lengthy legal analysis for the Commissioner of Indian Affairs of the question whether the Utes of the Uintah Valley Reservation in Utah were entitled to some of the benefits of the treaties made with Colorado Utes. Many Indian bands in Utah spoke the Ute language, and the 1868 treaty referred to a Uintah band. The conclusion of the analysis was that the 1873 Brunot negotiation, and the Act of June 15, 1880 approving and providing for implementation of the March,1880

---

81. Telegram French to the Secretary of Interior, December 15, 1880, NARA M234, Roll 214.
82. Telegram Schurz to French, Dec. 17, 1880, Sen. Exec. Doc. 31 (46-3), p. 39.
83. Telegram Schurz to French, Dec. 6, 1880, Sen. Exec. Doc. 31 (46-3), p. 38
84. Telegram Mears, French and Berry to Schurz, December, 1880, Sen. Exec. Doc. 31 (46-3), p. 38
85. Telegram Schurz to Berry, Dec. 20, 1880, NARA M234, Roll 213.

agreement on sale of the reservation concerned only the Ute Indians of Colorado.[86]

As 1881 opened, the Tabeguache knew that they would soon have to leave the Los Pinos agency on the Uncompahgre. But when, and precisely where they would move, was still unknown. The Utes did not like what they saw of the area along the Grand River near the mouth of the Gunnison first proposed for their new home. Lack of grass for their stock was the major complaint. A new delegation sent to Washington resulted in the Government proposing that the Tabeguache move to Utah as the White River Utes had already done. The *New York Times*, in referring to this proposal, spoke out for the Indians, editorializing: "The representatives of the Utes are in Washington, complaining that they had been cheated in the agreement by which they gave up nearly all of their Colorado lands. This is precisely what might have been expected. They were cheated. It has been the practice of our government, from time immemorial, to cheat the Indians whenever any treaty has been made with them. The Utes were first bullied, starved and menaced, and then bribed and cajoled. The Ute chiefs in Washington signed the agreement, but under protest. As soon as they had gone home, Congress deliberately hacked at it and patched it, until it was no longer what the Ute chiefs had accepted. Then there were more negotiations, and, as usual, the Indians finally gave in, and the amended agreement was once more signed. The Utes now complain that they have not left to themselves enough arable land for subsistence. The Secretary of the Interior blandly informs the complainants that the "treaty" must stand, and that if they have not enough land fit for cultivation, they may go to—Utah! It is the inexorable fate of the Indian that he shall be cheated in his dealings with white man. In this particular case, the Indian may consider himself lucky that he has escaped extermination at the hands of the brave and hardy freemen of Colorado. If the Utes had not given up their lands, they would have been driven out by a justly indignant white population, bent on occupying a tract which was merely useful as a means of subsisting Indians. This hardship they have escaped, and yet they are not happy."[87]

---

86. Undated and unsigned memorandum on stationary of the Department of the Interior, filed with 1880 material, NARA M234, Roll 214. This may have been prompted by a letter from John Critchlow, Agent at the Uintah Reservation in Utah, to W. L. Stickney of the Ute Special Commission which came West in 1878. Critchlow had asked that his charges benefit from the payments then being made. See Senate Executive Document 62 (45-3), Serial Set 1831.

87. *New York Times*, March 11, 1881, p. 4, column 1.

While these problems were being worked out, many in Colorado were impatient to move into the Ute lands. The August 20, 1881 edition of the *Pitkin Independent*, a weekly published in the mining town of Pitkin in Gunnison County, contained an editorial on the prospects for mining on those Ute lands. The editorial writer predicted that when the new country opened for settlement, the world would witness one of the most splendid exhibitions of rapid development ever known. He wrote that little hardship would be involved, for two railroads were ready to follow the tide as soon the doors opened. The same paper on Oct. 15, 1881 quoted the Gunnison *News Democrat* about parties of whites were waiting in town to go into the new lands.

Of course, not everyone waited for the Utes to leave, which did not happen until September, 1881. The Commandant at the Cantonment on the Uncompahgre reported to his headquarters in November, 1880 that the Los Pinos Utes were complaining about prospectors working along the Grand River.[88] The problem had become so acute by May, 1881 that Washington told the Los Pinos agent to give notice to trespassers on the reservation to leave within 7 days or face ouster by force. The Commandant then asked his superiors for instructions what to do if he were called on to assist the agent in this ouster.[89]

On August 22 at Los Pinos, Berry called the Utes in council and told them to prepare to move starting on August 25. Berry told them he would issue three weeks supplies for the trip, and that the agency and certain public property would be moved away immediately upon their departure. Interior would pay compensation to those Indians, immediately upon their arrival in Utah, who had made improvements in the Uncompahgre Valley. The Indians declined to leave. Among other things, they wanted to be paid for these improvements before they left. Berry then asked Colonel McKenzie, the Fort Crawford Commandant, to take charge and escorted the principal chiefs to see McKenzie. On learning that McKenzie was now in charge of them, and upon hearing him state that he preferred that the move be peaceable, they said they would go. McKenzie put Berry back in charge on August 26. On August 27, Berry issued the promised three weeks' rations, and the move began. McKenzie had large boats to be placed at the crossings of the Grand and Green Rivers so that Indians and their property could cross safely.

---

88. Letter Commandant at Fort Crawford to the Assistant Adjutant General, Department of the Missouri, Fort Leavenworth, Kansas, November 13, 1880, Crawford, p. 41.

89. Letter Commandant to the Assistant Adjutant General, Department of the Missouri, Fort Leavenworth, Kansas, May 3, 1881, Crawford, p. 137.

The buildings and property at the old agency were auctioned off August 29-31, with usable, moveable property and agency records sent by wagon to Gunnison. From there, these went by rail to Salt Lake City, whence by wagon, 210 miles through the mountains to the new site. Berry left Los Pinos September 3, arriving in Salt Lake City September 9. He found many goods and supplies for the new agency already there, and sent these a few days later to the new site. The Tabeguache were expected to arrive at the new site on September 20, 1881.[90] The 1881 Annual Report of the Commissioner of Indian Affairs discussed the end of the Los Pinos agency this way: "The commissioners appointed under the act of June 15, 1880 which ratified the Ute agreement of March 3, 1880 have selected a reservation near the confluence of the White and Green Rivers in Utah adjacent to the Uintah Indian reservation for the Uncompahgre Utes who formerly were located at the Los Pinos agency, Colorado. The Uncompahgre Utes have been removed thereto. The buildings of the former Los Pinos agency have been sold, and new ones have been erected at the new agency, which is called the Ouray agency in recognition of the friendship and faithfulness to the whites of Ouray, former head chief of the Utes."[91] Short shrift indeed for Chief Ouray.

Agent Berry's September 10, 1881 report from Salt Lake City stated that peaceful removal of Utes had been "accomplished successfully." He explained the failure to locate the Tabeguache along the Grand River as first contemplated. He said that in the latter part of May, Ute Commissioners Russell, Mears, and Judge McMorris arrived at Los Pinos. On June 10, the Commissioners, Berry and some chiefs went to the Grand River to see if the area was suitable for a new Ute home; it was instead found to be unsuitable. Then the group looked at the country along the Green, White, and Grand Rivers, which proved satisfactory. Berry noted that some of the Tabeguache had wanted to stay in the Uncompahgre Valley below Ouray's house, but these never said flatly that they would not move.

Ouray's widow, Chipeta, had wanted to stay in the house Ouray had built, but she was compelled to leave the Uncompahgre valley with the others. She evidently did not remain indefinitely on the new reservation in Utah. In 1887, some citizen groups in Colorado went on a campaign to expel some White River Utes who by then were back in Colorado, either on self-created homesteads or as herders in mountain valleys. On August 13, 1887, one of the herding Utes came to the reservation in Utah to complain that his tents near Meeker had been burned down, his goods pilfered, and six women and eight children had been kidnaped.

---

90. CIA, 1881, p. 14.
91. CIA, 1881, p. XLVI.

Chipeta seems also to have been a victim of this attack, losing some of the large herd inherited from Ouray.[92]

Removal of the Los Pinos and White River Utes to Utah was not all that Colorado citizens wanted. They also wanted the land of the former reservation put into the public domain so that they could start staking out claims and obtaining title to farms and ranches there. Typical of the agitation for early opening of the Ute lands was a mass meeting held in Gunnison in February, 1882.[93] Soon Colorado legislators on Capital Hill in Washington, addressing the need for further legislation to open the lands formerly occupied by the Uncompahgre and White River Utes public lands, introduced bills in the House[94] and Senate.[95] These resulted in a law approved July 28, 1882[96] making the old reservation lands part of the public domain subject to private claim under such regulations as the Secretary of Interior might establish. There was one restriction: former Ute Reservation land could only be sold, not disposed of for free under the Homestead Act. A minimum price of $1.25 per acre was set with the idea that the sales proceeds would go to raising the monies promised to the Utes.[97]

This 1882 law opening the Ute reservation to settlement contained a special provision (Section 3) legalizing certain claims made to the Ute Reservation before the lands were opened to claiming, contrary to the earlier Schurz declaration that no claim based on actions before reservation was officially open would be accepted. The Senate Committee Report justified this action as follows: "In 1879, the boundary line of the reservation not having been established by a survey, a large number of well disposed citizens, attracted by the reputed existence of rich mineral deposits, went upon lands which were afterwards found by survey to be upon the reservation. They established homes, built houses and churches, constructed roads, and expended many thousand dollars in prospecting for and in developing mines. The government of the United States, at that time, recognized the lands upon which these improvements were made as lying without the boundary of said reservation and lawfully open to settlement, and upon application by citizens then occupying the land, and upon payment therefor, caused the same to be surveyed and subdivided, and received applications in the United

92. CIA, 1887, pp. 76-80.
93. Senate Miscellaneous Document No. 63 (48-1), Serial Set 2173.
94. House Report No. 1304 (47-1), Serial Set 2069.
95. Senate Report No. 186 (47-1), Serial Set 2004.
96. 22 Stat. 178.
97. This restriction Congress canceled in 1902.

States land office for patents for portions of said lands. The Indians themselves disclaimed any right to these lands.

"By order of the Commissioner of the General Land Office, in 1881, certain portions of said lands were declared to be part of the Indian reservation and withdrawn from sale, and no filings or applications to purchase were allowed to be received at the local land office for any of the lands.

"Your committee is of the opinion that some provision should be made for the protection of the interest of these settlers."

This opinion was given despite a negative report from the Commissioner of Indian Affairs. The Commissioner questioned Section 3 of the proposed bill, providing that claims made in good faith to lands no more than 10 miles into the reservation would be considered valid. The Commissioner charged this would reward people who had jumped the gun. He wrote the Interior Secretary on Jan. 21,1882:

"In the view of this office, the government would stultify itself by the enactment of any law that might be construed as supporting protection to those who, in direct and flagrant violation of law, and in spite of the persistent efforts of the department to prevent them, had gone on and made settlement and location upon the lands in question.

"There are a very large number to purchase to whom the remarks apply directly. They are scattered all over the ceded lands, and such was the disorder and rapacity of their conduct during the negotiations in final removal of the Indians as to seriously in danger the peaceful and successful work of removal.

"They crowded in upon the Indians ere they had fairly vacated the lands they so dearly prized. Indeed, so close upon them that they must have witnessed, possibly not without some degree of shame, the touching evidences of the peculiar attachment of these people for their homes and country. It is related that when they had finally set out on their long march to their new homes in Utah, many of them repeatedly turned back, and kneeling, kissed the ground, no doubt bitterly lamenting their voluntary banishment."[98]

The Committee Report also enclosed a letter from Secretary of the Interior Samuel Kirkwood dated February 6, 1882. Kirkwood, about to resign to run for the Republican Presidential nomination in 1884, mildly endorsed Section 3 of the bill and tipped his hat in the direction of Colorado's two Republican Senators: "Before the east line of the Ute Reservation in Colorado was established, it was understood by both the Indians and the whites that the line was some miles

---

98.   House Report 1304 (47-1), Serial Set 2069.

west of where it was subsequently ascertained to be. Many white settlers, acting upon this understanding, and without objection on the part of the Indians, settled upon the strip of land which, when the true line was established, was found to be within the reservation; they made valuable improvements thereupon, are still there, and are naturally very anxious to have the validity of their claims duly established. This information is derived mainly from unofficial sources, but is confirmed by the senators from Colorado, who are familiar with the facts." Familiar with the facts, probably, but the Colorado Senators were hardly disinterested parties.

On April 18, 1882, Iowan Kirkwood was replaced as Secretary of the Interior by Henry M. Teller, a man with great interest in mining activities in his home state, and for whom later would be named Teller County in Colorado and the town of Teller in Alaska. Secretary Teller on May 10 wrote the House Committee considering the bill, saying that "the third section of the bill was intended to protect the occupation of a large number people, who, believing that the east line of the Ute Reservation to be several miles west of its real location, settled within the limits of the reservation. The Indians did not claim the settlements were within reservation, and the officials of the United States, supposing them to be without the reservation, allowed applications to be filed for the entry of mineral lands, which were duly surveyed by the Surveyor General of the state of Colorado. It was not discovered until after the passage of the Act of June 15, 1880 (which approved the agreement with the Utes by which they sold their reservation), that the settlements were in fact on the reservation. Much confusion has arisen since with reference to titles in the vicinity, and the third section is to protect a bona fide occupant in the improvements made under the circumstances aforementioned. The bill is a proper one, and ought to pass."[99] Because of Section 3, this law is sometimes called "The Ten Mile Strip Act."

The 1880 law on the sale of the Ute reservation did throw a bone in the direction of the Ute desire to keep settlers out of Uncompahgre Park, which had been restored to the Indians by President Grant's Executive Order in 1877. Section 8 of the 1880 law provided that "the hot springs in Uncompahgre Park, with the surrounding four mile square comprising the springs and the valley, are withdrawn from settlement and set apart for the enjoyment of the people." In 1884, with Ouray dead, a new law repealed this set aside.[100]

---

99. *ibid.*
100. 21 Stat. 199.

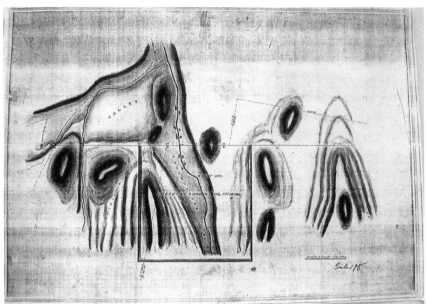

4 Mile Square Uncompahgre Park

So the squatters in Uncompahgre Park won, after all. Ouray's favorite spring, now known as the Orvis Spring, is open to who are willing to pay the fees that the commercial operator charges. One wonders whether the Ute lands would have been treated in this fashion if Ouray had not died in the summer of 1880. One also wonders too if the party sent to examine the lands at the junction of the Gunnison and Grand Rivers for suitability for settling the Tabeguache would, if Ouray had been part of it, have concluded the area lacked good pasturage for the Indians' livestock.

Orvis Spring, south of Ridgeway, CO

6

Ouray in Retrospect

The Southern Utes under Chief Ignacio had often opposed Ouray while he was alive. After his death, the Southern Utes became happy to honor him as a great leader. They have done so in many ways, including this fine stone monument.

Ouray Memorial, Southern Ute Reservation

Even if Ouray was not truly the "principal chief of the Ute nation," universally accepted as such during his life by all Colorado Utes, settlers in Colorado had reason to appreciate him as a good role model. And not just because Ouray believed that it was futile for the Utes to resist the massive inflow of whites into

Ute lands. No, Ouray also showed how far an Indian could go to adapt to the realities of the white man's world, the long range goal of Washington's Indian policy. For example, Ouray preferred living in a house rather than a teepee, managing, over the initial opposition of Agent Bond, to erect a substantial house about eight miles north of the agency proper. Bond's successor as agent, W. D. Wheeler, really admired Ouray, readily calling him the head chief of the Utes. Wheeler wrote that Ouray's dwelling house, together with other buildings for his use, had been completed only within a short time and was the most complete and substantial residence within the agency limits.

Ouray loved horse racing. He had a race track near his house and liked to hold races with many in attendance. In the spring of 1880, Ouray was in poor health, probably with the illness which would kill him within months and was evidently consulting the Agency doctor.[1] Although then troubled in body, and perhaps in mind, Ouray continued to play the role of a gregarious host by bringing Indians from several bands to his home to engage in his favorite sport of horse racing. Some 500 Tabeguache and White Rivers attended races there in May, 1880.[2] One reason for Ouray gave for wanting to hold on to Uncompahgre Park was that this land was needed for pasturing his horses.[3]

Ouray was at home in the white man's world. For example, long before the age of high priced media consultants, he realized the value of good relations with the Colorado public. Example: his efforts to put the Indian view point across to Coloradans in his 1873 letter to Felix R. Brunot for relay to white Coloradans. And in April, 1878, when the Utes were striving to have squatters expelled from the tract known as Uncompahgre Park (a tract promised to them in the Brunot Agreement and confirmed to them by an Executive Order of President Grant in 1876), Ouray addressed a letter to the "Generals, Colonels and Captains of the City of Ouray," stating that miners and settlers must keep off the reservation.[4] Also he understood how to negotiate a bank draft. Once when needing funds in Denver, Ouray sold to a Denver bank a draft on the Los Pinos agent for $50, which agent Bond accepted as moneys properly due Ouray as interpreter.[5] Fur-

---

1.   Letters Gilson to Colonel McKenzie, April 20, 1880, NARA M234, Roll 213, and April 23, 1880, Roll 214.
2.   Letter Gilson to Colonel McKenzie, May 17, 1880, NARA M234, Roll 214.
3.   Senate Executive Document 29 (46-2), Serial Set 1882, p. 90, hereafter simply Sen. Exec. Doc. 29 (46-2).
4.   Letter Ouray to an unknown resident of Ouray town, April 15, 1878, Sen. Exec. Doc. 29, p. 64.
5.   Letters Bond to the CIA, Dec. 29, 1874 and Jan. 4, 1875, NARA M234, Roll 205

ther, Ouray had an idea of white man's concepts of justice. At the hearings at Los Pinos in November, 1879 to determine the guilty parties in the Meeker killings and kidnapings, Ouray successfully asserted a Fifth Amendment right for accused Utes: no one should be forced to give testimony that might incriminate himself.[6]

Unlike most his fellows, Ouray appreciated the value of education. Without children in his own household, Ouray persuaded his nephew to spent a winter at the Los Pinos agency so as to enroll his children in the school.[7] Unfortunately, the nephew's wife took sick and the family instead spent the winter lower down in Saguache. Ouray with Chipeta went to visit the Carlisle Indian School in February, 1880 while in Washington to negotiate the sale of the Ute reservation. Interior Secretary Schurz approved the Carlisle visit first just for Ouray and four others; no doubt encouraged by Ouray, the accompanying Utes later grew to eleven.[8]

Ouray was happy to pose for the camera with his wife Chipeta. Photographer John Nicholas Choate of Carlisle, who made it his business to take pictures of Indian chiefs who visited the Indian School there, had Ouray and Chipeta sit for him in 1880. Matthew Brady of Civil War fame posed the two in his studio on Pennsylvania Avenue in Washington, D. C. on one of their earlier visits to the Nation's Capital. Brady ultimately went bankrupt and sold his collection of negatives to the Library of Congress for $25,000 in order to pay off his debts. Ouray's photographs show him as being not of great stature, perhaps five feet seven inches tall. While Ouray often dressed in white man's fashion, he always kept his hair in Ute fashion: long and in two braids that he wore on his chest.

Ouray showed an interest in agriculture not typical of the Utes of the time. During the summer of 1876, Ouray, assisted by Utes only, built a substantial fence around about 10 acres of land in the Uncompahgre Valley, a portion of which he then cultivated. Agent Bond subsequently told Washington that Ouray had been much pleased with the removal of the Agency to the Uncompahgre Valley where farming as possible, and that he would continue to farm.[9] Ouray's example evidently prompted another chief, Shavano, to take up farming.[10]

Now, the testimony of some whites who had known Ouray well, although these observations were put into writing only years after the events: Denver Spe-

---

6. Commission Proceedings for November 14, 1879, House Executive Document no. 83 (46-2), Serial Set 1925, p. 12.

7. Letter Bond to the CIA, Feb. 9, 1875, NARA M234, Roll 205.

8. Letter Schurz to the CIA, February 10, 1880, M606, roll 23, p 211.

9. Letter Bond to the CIA, CIA 1876, p. 20.

10. Letter Gilson to Colonel McKenzie, May 17, 1880, NARA M234, Roll 214.

cial Indian Agent James Thompson, Interior Secretary Carl Schurz, and Los Pinos employee Sidney Jocknick.

Territorial Governor McCook had brought his brother-in-law, Thompson, to Denver to work on Indian Affairs. Thompson acted as agent to the various Indian bands that came to Denver from time to time. Thompson said in an interview a half century later: "Ouray was a good man, who would have measured up to a high standard in any civilized community...He lived like a white man." But Thompson also gave an idea of how Ouray may have appeared to the Utes: "Ouray was an autocratic ruler who might summarily put to death any Indian who disobeyed his orders. Ouray was inexorable in his enforcement of the law as he understood it, but to his credit was most particular to establish the facts before proceeding with punishment."[11]

The officials who met Ouray on his visits to Washington were favorably impressed. Ouray's intellect was noted by all. Take Interior Secretary Schurz. During Ouray's stay in Washington in 1880, Schurz several times entertained Ouray in his home, and came to admire him. In his personal papers written late in life, Schurz said that Ouray "spoke like a man of a high order of intelligence and of larger views who had risen above the prejudices of his race, and expressed his thoughts in language clear and precise, entirely unburdened by the figures of speech and superfluous comment current among Indians.....Ouray was by far the brightest Indian I have ever met.[12] President Rutherford Hayes met Ouray and called him "the most intellectual man I've ever conversed with."[13]

Sidney Jocknick, the one time cook and herder at Los Pinos, left in a book published only in 1998 what I consider to be the most insightful and nuanced evaluation of Ouray made by anyone who had known him personally. Jocknick wrote that the Indians "in their intercourse with the Government had tacitly recognized Ouray as their leader, for the government would talk to no one else. For that matter, Ouray was the only Chief who could make himself understood in English. Being among his fellows, their interest dictated the above recognition, albeit it was a recognition that was responsible only to the white men, for as among themselves, they could not be persuaded to hail Ouray at once as their Chief. On the other hand, he was the only one among to them who had the abil-

---

11.   Thomas F. Dawson, "Major Thompson, Ouray and the Utes," _Colorado Magazine_, Vol. VIII, pp. 113-120.

12.   As quoted in Sidney Jocknick, _Early Days on the Western Slope of Colorado_, Ouray, Col., Western Reflections, 1998, pp. 228-229.

13.   Jocknick, _ibid._

ity and courage to cater to their interest, the only one with sagacity enough to see clearly their relative position as wards of the nation."

Ouray was so highly thought of by many later-year Coloradans that a local chapter of the Daughters of the American Revolution bought the land where Ouray's house had once stood and donated the land to the State of Colorado for a memorial. The Colorado Historical Society now operates the Ute Museum on that spot. Ouray and Chipeta are prominently featured in the Museum. Chipeta's remains were moved to the Museum site years after her death in Utah.

Tomb of Chipeta at Ute Museum

PART II
Porter Nelson

PORTER NELSON
Aspen, 1890

7

Working on the Railroad

On January 13, 1887, the Pueblo newspaper, *Colorado Chieftain*, alerted its readers that strangers were in town. In an article headed "Santa Fe Road to Have a North Branch," the paper wrote: "The community was agreeably startled on Sunday night when news began to circulate that a party of railroad surveyors had arrived in town. Nobody knew anything for certain about them, but yesterday they couldn't altogether conceal what they were about.

"There were nine surveyors in the outfit. They arrived at noon on Sunday from Topeka, and have taken lodging and board at the Purple House, on Second Street. They also secured Room 13 in the Holden block, on Santa Fe Avenue, as an office and temporary headquarters. The two who seem to direct things are Messrs. Kelly and Follett. They have employed two men named Rosenfield and Duncan in the city, the one as a teamster and the other as a helper, their engagements being for two months.

"Yesterday morning the core of surveyors got out their tripods and glasses and began work, evidently by instructions already well planned. They commenced laying out a line, beginning in the extreme end of the Santa Fe switch yards. They left the mainline of the Santa Fe Road at the point where the water runs into the upper City Reservoir, then proceeded almost due north, past Josiah Hugh's residence, east of the insane asylum grounds, thence across the open tract belonging to the Masonic fraternity, on past the Cemetery, going immediately to the east of it. Thence the way is clear to the Fountain (Creek).

"These gentlemen have nothing to say to inquirers, and have strict instructions to give nobody any information as to their affairs. It is very plain that they are in the service of Santa Fe Co., and it can easily be conjectured that they will survey a line to Colorado Springs and Denver. To this anybody's imagination can attach anything they wish. The probability of a connection with Colorado Midland seems very strong."

Railroads were expanding all across the country in the 1880's, just as "dot-com's" did in the 1990's. And the Santa Fe was known in Colorado as one of the strong contenders for the future rail traffic of that expanding state. The Santa Fe headquartered in Topeka, and the Denver and Rio Grande Western based in Denver, were great rivals. The Santa Fe beat its Colorado rival in the contest to be the first to put rails across Raton Pass into New Mexico. In the year 1878, these two railroads started a battle to be the first to build a line through the Royal Gorge of the Arkansas River to reach the mining area around Leadville. For a time, the Santa Fe leased the whole Rio Grande system. On February 2, 1880, the Santa Fe and the Rio Grande settled their arguments out-of-court, in the so-called "Treaty of Boston." The Santa Fe gave up its lease of the Rio Grande, and all litigation stopped. In 1882, the Santa Fe obtained Rio Grande consent to run Sante Fe trains from Pueblo to Denver over the Rio Grande line by laying a third rail outside the latter's narrow gauge tracks. This operation became increasingly difficult. In 1887, the Missouri Pacific Railroad was completing a rail line from Kansas into Pueblo, threatening existing traffic arrangements in Colorado. Fearing loss of traffic to the newcomer, the Santa Fe decided to build its own standard gauge track 116 miles north from Pueblo to Denver. This is what brought the Santa Fe survey party to Pueblo in January, 1887.

The Rio Grande was not the sole Colorado-based railroad at this time feverishly building lines from the eastern foothills into the mountains to tap the traffic coming from the many new mines being opened in Colorado. The Colorado Midland Railroad also was pushing west, from its base in Colorado Springs. Early in 1888, the Midland put a standard gauge line into Aspen, building a costly and difficult-to-keep-open tunnel through the Continental Divide. On September 5, 1890, the Santa Fe announced it's purchase of the 327 mile long Colorado Midland Railway, to prevent either the Rio Grande or the Rock Island from buying that railroad and diverting traffic away from the Santa Fe. A bad purchase. The Colorado Midland never made money and showed few signs of ever doing so. In 1896, after the repeal of the Sherman Silver Purchase Act crippled the silver mining industry, the Santa Fe wrote off its Midland investment and let it go its own way.

The *Chieftain* article did not say it, but one of the mysterious party of Santa Fe surveyors was a 24 year old Virginian, W. Porter Nelson. Nelson was my maternal grandfather, a Civil War child born in April, 1862 in the family of a well-to-do merchant in the market town of Culpeper. He had graduated from Roanoke College in Salem, Virginia in 1882, studying liberal arts but excelling in mathematics. It was probably his proficiency in mathematics, and possibly good family connections, which enabled him to be part of the Santa Fe Railroad survey party in Pueblo in January, 1887. This was Nelson's first work for an employer other than his father.

The *Chieftain* article did note that the two men hired in Pueblo were given contracts for just 2 months. Porter Nelson did not work on the Sante Fe survey very long either. When at the end of January, he got his first meager pay from the railroad, a draft for less than $1, he saved the draft as a souvenir. The draft was found among his papers after his death in 1946. By May, 1887, articles in Culpeper newspapers were reporting on his activities back in Virginia.[1] Long railroad employment or not, 20 years later a newspaper in the silver mining city of Aspen of Colorado would describe Nelson as having at that time done responsible work "behind the transit." More importantly, Nelson's brief experience in blossoming Colorado of the 1880's left him with a desire to "get in on the action" there. He did come back to Colorado, in 1888, this time to settle down. He appeared in Aspen early that year with money to spend, and made a number of investments. In February, 1888, he recorded purchase of one town property in Aspen, in March one more, in April six more. In the June-July period, he made chattel loans to two local business men.

Growing up, Porter Nelson had learned from his father about forming companies, buying real estate, and such. But nothing to do with mining. He had not even studied geology or joined the mineralogy club when he attended Roanoke College in Virginia. Nelson's expenditures in Aspen in early 1888 did not include mining properties. Money invested in real estate, Nelson went back East where he married a Baltimore belle in September, to bring her to Aspen to establish a permanent residence and raise a family. Not clear whether he used the Rio Grande or the Midland railroad in his travels to and from Aspen.

Where did he get all the money he was putting into these investments? In all probability, he had persuaded his father, Lewis Porter Nelson, to finance him in Colorado as sort of an early inheritance. His father was primarily a merchant, but also an investor in Virginia real estate, a bank, a turnpike company, and other similar activities. When Porter Nelson in September came back to Aspen with his bride, the former Julia Henry Blackwell of Baltimore, he evidently still had some money to invest. Perhaps it was Julia Henry who encouraged Porter to go into mining, as on coming back to Aspen with her, he began to put money there, too.

---

1.   An article in the Culpeper paper *Star Exponent* of October 14, 1887 referred to a Culpeper partnership in which Porter Nelson was involved.

8

Carry Me Away from Old Virginny

People who in the early years brought outside capital into Colorado to invest in the state's development were considered heroes of a sort. Porter Nelson was not a big time investor, certainly not in the same league as Aspen big timers like Jerome B. Wheeler, a former partner in the R. H. Macy Company of New York, or Cincinnati lawyer David B. Hyman, who also made a splash in Aspen. But an Aspen newspaper in 1907 credited Nelson with bringing into Colorado over the years as much as $250,000 of investment money, thus making him a hero of a sort. Much of this money came from relatives back in Virginia, or elsewhere.

The main source of his funds, initially at least, was his father, Lewis Porter Nelson. Porter's relationship with his father was a complicated one. Porter was the eldest son born of the father's third marriage, but not the father's first-born son. That first-born son was Porter's half brother, Lucian Mortimer Nelson. Lucian was the first of Lewis's sons to leave the family nest, and perhaps set a pattern. Lucian's departure, after his graduation from the University of Virginia, was easy to understand. His mother had died when he was an infant, and Lewis Porter Nelson had gone on to build a large family with his third wife. Lucian Nelson went off to central Missouri, to which Virginia Nelsons had been moving for some time. He married a local girl, and helped found the town of Nelson in Saline County, Missouri.

Porter Nelson's own move away from a prospective easy existence in Virginia is not so easy to comprehend. He may have feared falling victim to tuberculosis, as happened with several of his siblings, namely George, Arthur and Kate. Also, his father, Lewis Porter Nelson, had a reputation as a hard man to work for. Lewis Porter may have viewed son William Porter as an impractical dreamer who should be allowed to leave. Whatever, when he had only one son left at home, the Nelson patriarch was determined not to let namesake Lewis Porter Nelson, Jr.

flee the nest. Junior had to stay on to manage Nelson property after the old man's death.

Patriarch Lewis Porter Nelson was the first of his Nelson line to go into business instead of agriculture, starting out in business with a country store along a major road in the Madison district of Culpeper County.

First Store and Home of Lewis Porter Nelson
Madison County, Virginia

As his business prospered, Lewis Porter Nelson subsequently moved his business into the nearest big town, the county seat and market town of Culpeper. He earned a reputation as a sharp businessman and became an investor in a number of enterprises. After the Civil War, he was one of the largest landowners in Culpeper County.

Lewis Porter Nelson died in Culpeper in March, 1906. His long handwritten will dated shortly before his death says a lot about his relationship with son Porter who had gone off to Colorado in 1888. The first three clauses of this will appointed his namesake son and one son-in-law as executors, directed that all his debts be paid off promptly, and provided for his wife, Mary Elizabeth Nelson. The fourth clause directed that his remaining real and personal property be divided into six more or less equal packages and distributed by the drawing of lots to named parties. One package was to go to his namesake son. One package each was to go to male trustees for his daughters, Lizzie, Maggie Belle and Lucille. One package was to go to trustees for the children of his deceased first born son, Lucian, who were then living in Pueblo, Colorado with their remarried mother and her second husband. The final package was to go his remaining living child, Porter Nelson, but only to him as trustee for his three children. This suggests a certain reserve on the part of Lewis towards son Porter.

The fifth clause of the will contained rules for the trustees' management of the property put in trust for his daughters. The sixth clause of the father's will gives more insight into the father's relationship with son Porter. While Lewis Porter Nelson had advanced money to a number of his children, it is only with regard to William Porter Nelson that Lewis Porter's will lists specific bonds covering money advanced before the father's final illness. William Porter's bonds were listed as:

May 29, 1886	$5,000
May 15, 1888	$3,000
July 1, 1888	$1,400
October 11, 1888	$1,000
July 1, 1889	$1,500
January 9, 1894	$3,300
March 15, 1894	$1,000

This clause also cited a bond for $1,000 dated June 29, 1888 given by Porter Nelson to J. J. Roberts, payment of which Lewis Porter Nelson had guaranteed, and also a $1,500 note given by Porter Nelson to uncle Arthur B. Nelson dated January 1, 1892, which Lewis Porter Nelson had acquired. Also a note for $5,000 which Porter Nelson had given his father around the year 1900 when he needed money for himself and his children. And $1,849.93, being one fifth part of payments due on a mortgage of property in Kaufman County, Texas which Lewis Porter Nelson had directed his brother-in-law, James S. Grinnan of Terrell, Texas, to pay to son Porter Nelson as they came in. Lewis Porter's will totaled the father's advancements to son Porter at $25,569.93, a sum which Lewis noted did not include interest. As a generous gesture, Lewis Porter commuted the total amount owed by son Porter to only $21,149.93.

Lewis Porter noted that, since he had advanced $12,000 to each of his other children, Porter would have to pay interest only on the excess of this amount, namely $9,149.93. Interest on this remainder, at 6 percent, was to be calculated only from January 1, 1901. A further sign of magnanimity: Lewis Porter Nelson said that if his listing of advances to son Porter was found to be not all inclusive, he did not want any omission to be added to the sum owed by Porter. The will shows what a tight-fisted businessman Lewis Porter Nelson was, carrying over for years that 93 cents that son William Porter Nelson. It also shows that Porter Nelson had received considerable money (in terms of 1880's dollars) from his father, money which no doubt helped finance Porter's early operations in Colorado.

Lewis Porter Nelson Family
Culpeper, 1901

The 6 percent interest on almost $10,000 from January 1, 1901 that Porter Nelson owed to the estate amounted to about $3,000. But probation of the will did not put Porter Nelson into a big financial hole. The 1/6th share of Lewis Porter Nelson's property that Porter Nelson drew by lot for his children under the fourth clause of the will, a package including the former family residence in downtown Culpeper, was valued at almost $17,000. So Porter Nelson did get control of some additional money on his father's death, but not much. He would be treated more generously under the will of his mother when she died in 1917.

Mary Elizabeth Nelson bequeathed a full third of her estate to son Porter, whereas her remaining heirs were given just 1/6th of her estate. But by 1917 when Mary Elizabeth died, Porter was no longer wheeling and dealing in Aspen.

9

In Real Estate, It's Not Just Location

One of Porter Nelson's biggest deals in the first years of his residence in Aspen was to buy a good building, in the best of locations, in then prosperous downtown Aspen. He bought the building, the Cowenhoven and Brown-built Aspen Block at 303 South Galena Street, mostly on hopes for the future but also to secure a prime address for his office. Nelson paid $45,000 for this building in 1890, at the peak of the Aspen boom. Messrs. Cowenhoven and Brown were then, or soon would be, Aspen's richest men. They did not attain that status by being on the losing side in many business deals; they did not mar their record in this deal, either. In the sale, they made 50 percent on their investment in just 4 years!. The value of Nelson's Aspen Block dropped quickly after the government stopped buying silver on the 1893 repeal of the Sherman Silver Purchase Act.

The Aspen Block

While Nelson did get others to buy shares in the Aspen Block, including a Nelson relative who was a well-to-do St. Louis banker, the purchase was a mistake. Some 17 years after his purchase, this would be cited in an Aspen paper, *The Aspen Democrat*, as a an example of Nelson's bad luck. The Aspen Block was a fine building, but the buy was a financial mistake. Still, Nelson could be proud to have his office in the Aspen Block at 303 Galena Street.

Of course, Porter Nelson was involved in many other real estate deals in Aspen. Some for his own account, and some while acting as escrow agent. One interesting Aspen deed record shows that on May 29, 1891, Nelson sold to Norman Ashby of Culpeper, Virginia "the full, free and perpetual right to dig, work, and search for minerals and remove all ore or mineral-bearing rock" underlying several town lots Nelson owned in the city of Aspen. Norman Ashby was the brother-in-law of Edgar Stallard, who worked closely with Porter Nelson in Aspen and also had his office in the Aspen Block. Edgar Stallard notarized the signature of Porter Nelson on the deed to Ashby. Under U. S. and Colorado law, the owner of mineral rights had the right to go after any minerals found there, and the owner of the surface rights must accommodate this work. It seems unlikely that Ashby wanted to do any mining. Indeed, given the geology of the city of Aspen's location, it is unlikely that any minerals could be mined there economically. It is more likely that Ashby took the deed as security for loan to Nelson.

Porter Nelson's Business Card

Porter Nelson, for all his buying and selling of town real estate, did not buy a family home in Aspen until years after his arrival. When he won election as Mayor of Aspen in 1897, he was living in his second rental house, this at 215 West Hallam Street. When he finally did buy a home for his family, he moved further out on West Hallam to No. 525. The previous owners of that house had been officers in Jerome B. Wheeler's bank. Nelson presumably got a good price when he bought, Aspen then being in decline. When he left Aspen in 1910, he thought he had managed to sell the house Dr. H. W. Twining, the County Medical Officer. But Aspen tax records, after listing Twining as owner of the house and showing Twining as paying the taxes thereon for the year 1911, record Pitkin County as buying the house from Nelson later, presumably for nonpayment of taxes. But Nelson had not come to Aspen just to dabble in town real estate. No, it was mineral wealth which had brought him West

10

It's the Minerals, Stupid!

Aspen was not the first Colorado silver mining boom town. Silvercliff was a silver boom town in the early 1870's, drawing enough population to justify formation in 1877 of Custer County out of southern Fremont County. Miners came to Leadviille for gold first, but by the early 1870's, that town too had become a major silver center. About the same time, prospectors trespassing on the Ute reservation found promising strikes of silver ore in Colorado's San Juan Mountains. So many, in fact, that the U. S. went back on its promise in the 1868 treaty that this area would be reserved for the Ute Indians in perpetuity. Although Aspen was east of the 107th meridian set in the 1868 treaty as the eastern boundary of the Ute reservation and thus was not off limits to miners after 1868, prospectors did not come to Aspen not until much later. Unlike in other districts, many ore finds around Aspen were not chance discoveries of lonely prospectors roaming about with wild hopes, guided only by instinct. No, the Hayden Geographical and Geological Survey had mapped the Aspen area in 1873-74, and its sixth report published in 1874 noted promising prospects in the upper valley of the Roaring Fork River. Prospectors began arriving in Aspen area in the summer of 1879, many presumably lured by these Hayden reports.

Two men who were not prospectors but investors and who never settled permanently in Aspen did much to shape Aspen's development. Most important was Jerome B. Wheeler, a New Yorker and one-time partner in the R. H. Macy Company. Wheeler, who arrived on the scene in 1883, has been credited with bringing $500,000 of Eastern money into the Aspen area. He was a builder, opening an opera house in Aspen in the spring of 1889 and the fine Hotel Jerome in the fall of that year. The second nonresident mover and shaker bringing in Eastern money was David Hyman, a lawyer in Cincinnati. Hyman was represented on the spot by Charles Hallam.

By 1885, serious mining development was underway in Aspen. In that year, limited electricity and telephone service began there. The first municipal school was constructed. One of major mines was sending by horse-drawn wagon as much as 15 tons of ore a day out of Aspen to smelters in Leadville and elsewhere at year end. The Denver and Rio Grande Railroad completed a narrow gauge line up the Roaring Fork River valley into Aspen in November, 1887. The standard gauge Colorado Midland Railroad completed its own line into Aspen just three months later.

So when Porter Nelson brought his bride to Aspen, it was no longer just a rough mining camp but verging on a real city. In October, 1888, presumably encouraged by new wife Julia Henry, Porter began to put some money into mining. He bought a 1/10th interest in the Abington and 1/6th interest in the Stilwell Lode claims. In November, he bought a 1/4 interest in the Sloven Lode claim in the Columbia district. He set himself up as an adviser on mining and other investments. There were many novices going into mining at the time. His first big move into mining came in 1890 when he took over claims filed by Virginia A. Funk and J. F. Gooding for finds named Springfield, Hayti, Havana, Borneo and R. G. in the Quartz Creek Mining District of Gunnison County. Nelson on April 11, 1890 used a Gunnison newspaper to publish the required public notice of his intent to patent these claims. This notice brought forth a law suits against the validity of the claims. The last challenge to the claims would be dismissed by the Federal District Court in Gunnison on December 8, 1890. Also on December 8, the clerk of the District Court in Gunnison County signed a certificate that there were no actions of any kind pending in that Court against the various claims, except for one which had been dismissed from the docket.

On the same day, Porter Nelson moved to get a patent on the claims. He swore at the Land Office in Gunnison, Colorado that since August 30, 1890 he had not filed mining claims on more than 320 acres. The Land Office in Gunnison acknowledged receipt of Nelson's payment in full for the land claimed, $285 for the 56.293 acres.[1] There were other costs, which Nelson had earlier met from his own pocket: $300 for an official survey of the claims; $35 to publish in a local paper for a period of 30 days the required public notice. He also presumably had to pay the cost of fighting off the challenge to the claims which the Gunnison court dismissed in 1890. Borneo patent no. 20766 was issued to him on April 23, 1892.

---

1.   The 1872 law set the price for mineral land at $5 per acre.

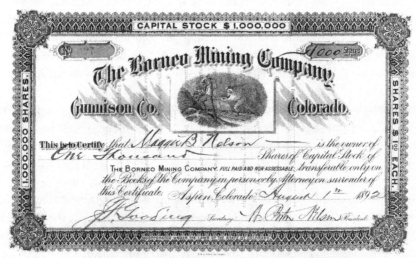

Borneo Mining Company Stock Certificate

Before the Borneo patent was granted, Nelson formed the Borneo Mining Company under Colorado law, filing a certificate to this effect in the Pitkin County Court House on July 2, 1891. The company was to sell stock to raise money to exploit the ores in these claims. The shares were priced at $1 each, and up to a million shares could be issued. The certificates for shares were lithographed by a Denver company. Nelson made himself president of the Borneo Mining Company and John Gooding became the Secretary. It is unclear how many invested in the Borneo Company, but one who did was Nelson's sister, Maggie Belle, back in Virginia. She received a certificate for 1,000 shares issued August 1, 1892. The Borneo Company lost money for its investors.

Porter Nelson obtained patents on two other mineral claims jointly with John F. Gooding and Virginia A Funk. One of these was for the Ben Hur and Gallion lodes, also in the Quartz Creek Mining District. Patent 21474 was issued for these on June 23, 1892. Nelson held a 3/8 share here, Gooding and Funk 1/4 each, and a John Currie and D.T. Reynolds held 1/12 each. Gooding and Funk were also involved in getting patent no. 26785 issued April 8, 1896 for the Lucky Queen lode in Pitkin County. One of the 1887 discoverers of this small (2.4 acre) lode was a George F. Bancroft, who had disappeared by the time Porter Nelson undertook to seek a patent on it. The 1900 census shows a J. F. Gooding living in Buena Vista, Colorado, whose occupation was given as "mining." In connection with another patent application involving Gooding and Virginia A.

Funk, the latter had to certify that she was an American citizen. Here she stated that she had been born in Virginia in 1852 and was residing in Aspen in 1887 when she and Gooding applied for that patent, on the Virginia Pet Lode in the Roaring Fork Mining District. Porter Nelson was not yet in Aspen and had nothing to do with this patent application. Patent no. 25265 for this claim was approved on February 2, 1895.

With other persons, Nelson received patent no. 20792 on April 23, 1892 for the Joe Dandy and a number of other lodes in Pitkin County. He also obtained patent no. 26326 on December 19, 1895 for the Last Chance Lode in Pitkin County, an appropriate name in view of Aspen's decline. Significant co-patentees on this 4.4 acre lode were capitalist Jerome B. Wheeler, and H. T. Tissington, a partner and cashier at the J. B. Wheeler Bank. None of these patents brought Nelson much wealth.

Most of Nelson's mining activity was focused on mines around the town of Crystal, in Gunnison County but not far as the crow flies west of Aspen. Far enough, though, that Crystal was west of the 107th meridian, and thus in that part of Colorado which from 1868 to 1882 belonged to the Ute reservation. It lies in the valley of the Crystal River, some 6 miles upstream from the town of Marble. The Crystal River was first called Rock Creek, and the whole mineral area became known as the Rock Creek Mining District. Prospectors first came into this district from Crested Butte. Active mining started above Crystal, by the short-lived town of Schofield even while it was part of the Ute reservation. But when Nelson arrived in Aspen, Crystal had become the hub of activity in the Rock Creek Mining District. A daily journal kept from 1886 to 1895 by a real hard rock miner, Frank Edgerton,[2] about doings in mining town of Crystal provides some insight into how Porter Nelson worked to put money to work in developing mineral prospects. Edgerton in his journal wrote particularly of Nelson's work in forming the Bear Mountain Company to develop mining claims that Edgerton controlled with two associates. This before the 1893 repeal of the Sherman Silver Purchase Act cut the price of silver.

Edgerton's entry for Dec. 2, 1890[3] stated that he was expecting Nelson with associates to create a stock company taking over three different groups of Edger-

---

2. The Colorado Historical Society has a transcription of the Edgerton journal. The 1900 census of Colorado recorded a 42 year old "quartz miner" named A. J. Edgerton as living in the town of Marble, a few miles downstream from Crystal, with a 24 year old wife named Hattie. No Frank Edgerton appeared in that census in Crystal or Marble.

3. Transcription of Edgerton daily journal, page 134.

ton-controlled claims. Seven claims were for the Illinois, five for the Paymaster, and three for a tunnel serving all these. This made 15 claims in all. Edgerton grandiosely proposed that Nelson issue 2,000,000 shares of stock valued at $100 per share. Of these, 750,000 shares would be divided between Edgerton and his associates, Melton and Lyons. Nelson and his partner in this plan would get 400,000 shares. The claims were for what later was known as the Bear Mountain properties. Edgerton's entry for December 12, 1890 states that he spent most of the day in Aspen with Nelson and his associate, and even went to the opera![4]

Edgerton's entry for December 18, 1890 records that Nelson's associate came to Crystal with Nelson's counterproposal for the Bear Mountain properties. This called for 2,000,000 shares of stock with a $1 per share par value. Edgerton, Lyons, and Melton would get 750,000 shares. Nelson and his associate were to get 500,000 shares. Nelson would guarantee sales of at least 3,000 shares of stock, from which $1,000 each would go to Edgerton and his associates. Nelson proposed that the company board consist of seven directors, with Edgerton, Lyons and Melton to be three. Nelson would name three directors, and his associate one.

Edgerton and his associates did not accept this proposal, and countered with the demand that they name four of the seven directors. To move the deal along, the Edgerton signed an escrow deed for the properties, which Nelson's associate took back to Aspen. Edgerton gave Nelson 60 days to respond to this counteroffer.[5] In January, Edgerton and associates gave Nelson an extension of time to reply, to March 8, 1891.[6] Edgerton noted in his journal of March 8, 1891 that he had still not received a reply from Nelson.[7]

Somehow, Nelson did reach agreement with Edgerton. Edgerton's entry for March 29, 1892 records that Nelson took a dozen samples and that Nelson told him that he was taking steps to have stock lithographed so sale of the certificates could begin. Nelson also told Edgerton that the payment of $1,000 each to him and his associates was due June 1. But Nelson said that payment for their expenses to date would be made only after the stock was actually sold. Nelson would let Edgerton and his associates hold Nelson's stock in escrow to guarantee payment.[8]

---

4.   *Op. Cit.*, p. 135.
5.   *Op. Cit.*, p. 136.
6.   *Op. Cit.*, p. 143.
7.   *Op. Cit.*, p. 145.
8.   *Op. Cit.*, p. 147.

Edgerton noted in his April 6, 1892 entry that Nelson's associate was in town, going up to the Illinois claim to take more samples, while bringing early sample results. One sample had showed 125 ounces of manganese per ton. Lead showed up in other samples.[9] On May 7, Edgerton noted that Nelson had come to Crystal to look again at the Illinois claim, bringing with him an expert named Ruse.[10] Edgerton's entry for New Year's Day, 1893 reported that he and one of his associates had gone to Aspen to see Nelson, who actually met them at the Leggetts Station on the Crystal River line.[11] His entry for January 2, 1893, reports reaching a deal with Nelson for the Illinois mine.[12] Edgerton's journal contains several later entries simply recording Nelson's presence in Crystal.

Now, some side bars to the Edgerton journal. In January, 1896, the Aspen newspaper *Rocky Mountain Sun* reported that Porter Nelson, the President of the Bear Mountain Mining Company, had returned to Aspen from 2 weeks in Crystal where he had let a contract for constructing a tunnel to develop various ore bodies there. He also brought with him 50 pounds of ore samples; some shipments of ore from Bear Mountain tested 92 ounces of silver per ton.

The Ruse who Edgerton noted as coming to Crystal with Nelson in May was a one-time assayer in Aspen who moved to greener pastures in Nevada when Aspen went down hill. In a decision handed down in September, 1908, the Pitkin County Court ruled that Porter Nelson had to pay $1,997.16 to the same Joseph Ruse, then in Esmeralda, Nevada. This judgement was recorded in Record Book 8. Unfortunately, the record book has been lost showing exactly what the suit concerned. Nelson did not satisfy Ruse on this judgement until 1917. Then Nelson was living in Denver and the price of mining stocks had risen due to World War I. Nelson paid off the judgement by turning over many shares of penny mining stocks: 10,000 shares of the Cumberland Consolidated Mining Company; 7,500 shares of the Marion Golden Mining and Milling Co.; 6,000 shares of the Monte Christo Consolidated Mining and Milling Co.; 13,500 shares of the Aspen Silver Mining Company; 6,000 shares of Hunter Creek Mining Company; 2,2 00 shares of the Justice Mining Company; 8, 571 shares of the U.S. Paymaster Mining Company; 15,000 shares of the Capitan Gold Mining Company; 2,250 shares of the West Aspen Mountain Mining Company; 5,000 shares of the Canterbury Mining Company; 1,000 shares of Nolan Creek; 21,875 shares of Vernon Consolidated Mines; 25,000 shares of the Portland

---

9.   *Op. Cit.,* p. 148.
10. *Op. Cit.,* p. 148.
11. *Op. Cit.,* p. 155.
12. *Op. Cit.,* p. 155.

Luning Copper Co.; 15,000 shares of the B. P. O. E. Mining Company; 5,000 shares of the Monivedo Mining and Milling Company; 6,000 shares of the World's Fair Mining and Milling Co.; and $100 in gold coin of the United States. The large number of shares which Nelson turned over to Ruse shows the extravagant hopes of those created these mining ventures, as well as those who bought shares in them, ventures which in the end turned out to be virtually worthless. Judging from the stock certificate for the 1,000 shares of the Borneo Mining Company which Nelson sold to his sister, Maggie Belle, the stock certificates for all these mining companies were not expensively printed in the East from engraved plates, but rather by a lithographer in Denver. If certificates for these companies still exist, they probably would not be deemed examples of high class scripophily.

Although Porter Nelson had not formally studied law before coming to Colorado, he had quickly picked up so much knowledge about the requirements of Colorado company law that he was able to serve as permanent secretary or other key officer of mining companies active around Aspen, and many near the town of Crystal. Some these companies, in addition to the Bear Mountain Tunnel and Mining Company and the Borneo Mining Company where Nelson was founder-President, included the North Pole Mining Company, the Lucky Boy Mining Company, the Aspen Mining Prospecting and Development Company, the Inez Mining Company, the Sheep Mountain Tunnel and Mining Company, the Colorado Highland Marble Company, and the Meadow Mountain Mining Company. He kept many of these companies on life support after others had given up all hope for them. Among his papers when he died were important records of these once promising companies.

Take the Meadow Mountain Mining Company as an example. This company was financed largely by investors from the state of Maine, few of whom seemed to have great familiarity with mining in Colorado. That company surprisingly was formed after the 1893 repeal of the Sherman Silver Purchase Act which caused a sharp downturn in silver mining centers such as Aspen. Porter Nelson was an officer in this company at least from 1903 to 1926, and seems by 1940 to control the property of that company as the sole surviving active officer. One of the properties of this company was the Lead King Mine above Crystal. In 1896, the Lead King yielded the largest galena nugget seen in Gunnison County, weighing 1,800 pounds. Porter Nelson's involvement with the Lead King came much later, but the early history of the Lead King mine provides interesting insights into mining around Crystal.

Town of Crystal in its Heyday

George H. Tays, Winfield S. Smith and Antoine R. Burnett, three residents of Crystal, filed affidavits on October 28, 1895 stating that they had located the Lead King Lode August 20, 1895. They filed a certificate of having done the requisite $100 worth of assessment work, which involved digging another 40 feet through solid rock. They came across a rich pocket of ore which yielded the super sized nugget mentioned above. Encouraged by this rich pocket, Tays, Burnett and Smith decided to patent the Lead King mine, and an associated 5 acre mill site as permitted by U.S. law. They picked the mill site on August 19, 1896 and had the lode and the mill site surveyed in November, 1896. They published the requisite public notice of intent to patent in the newspaper *Marble Times* early in 1897. The Land Office branch at Glenwood Springs approved their patent application on April 21, 1897. Patent no. 28425 was granted them on August 4, 1897, for the 9.3 acres of the lode, plus 5 acres for the mill site. An unusually short period here between location of the lode and issuance of the patent.

Six years later, Tays and Burnett sold to Porter Nelson as trustee, for the sum of $20,000, the patented Lead King mine and its 5 acre patented mill site, and also the lode claims known as the Tillman, and Silver King nos. 1 through 4. Tays and Burnett appeared before the Clerk of Gunnison County on August 20, 1903 to acknowledge their signature on the deed to Nelson. In Aspen on August 26, 1903, Porter Nelson as trustee acknowledged before his Notary Public colleague and fellow Virginian, Edgar Stallard, his signature on a deed transferring the same properties to the Meadow Mountain Mining Company, for the sum of $35,000.

The Meadow Mountain Mining Company which took over the Lead King mine from Nelson was not a great success. On January 21, 1913, the company directors meeting in Aspen approved reorganization of the Company and adopted a resolution as follows:

> Resolved—that the Treasurer of the Meadow Mountain Mining Company be, and he is hereby, authorized to issue the promissory notes of the company bearing the date of Jan. 1, 1913, to the persons and for the several amounts specified in the following list: each note when issued to the person named in the same to be delivered only upon the surrender to and cancellation by the Treasurer of any and all notes or other evidences of indebtedness held by the payee against the Company: such notes so issued shall bear interest at the rate 12 percent per annum and be payable by distribution pro rata among the several holders thereof from the funds of the Company by vote of directors from time to time as the funds in the Treasury of the Company may warrant: viz.

F. O. Beal	$4,135.00
John C. Bowling	1,208.34
Charles W. Coffin	421.35
John G. Dunning	122.95
George W. Dunning	22.95
W. L. Hunt	287.48
W. Porter Nelson	386.60
A. B. Haskell	559.82
Viktor Brett	384.33
A J. Waterman	262.55
E. F. Pember	389.09
J. M. Merrill estate	320.96
H. O. Pierce	34.10
T. W. Burr	13.40
C. J. Stewart heirs	82.00

On September 16, 1913, the Directors declared a dividend of 10 percent payable to the holders of the above notes, which was paid. The meeting notes stated that "the dividend was paid when the mine was operating at a fair price for the ore product, which indicates that it is still a good property."

This note suggests that some directors had doubts about the value of the Company. The interest rate of 12 percent on the Company's notes bespeaks of a risky security. The increase in metals prices in anticipation of war in Europe may have caused the "fair price" for company ores, particularly from the Lead King. The 10 percent dividend declared September 16, 1913 may well have been the first return the Meadow Mountain investors had seen for some time.

In 1920, Porter Nelson worked out a deal for new investors from Chicago to buy up Meadow Mountain shares in exchange for stock in a new company, to be called the Gold Reserve Company. The new company would take over the Meadow Mountain properties, and operate these in conjunction with Nevada mines the Chicagoans held. The Chicagoans would also issue 20,000 shares in the new company in exchange for the outstanding Meadow Mountain debt. The new Gold Reserve Company was to be capitalized at $5,000,000, or much more than the value of Meadow Mountain. Nelson's contact with the Maine investors, Victor Brett, liked the idea, reasoning that if the Gold Reserve stock to be received on exchange would be worth just 50 cents a share, this would about make up for all the money the Maine group had put into Meadow Mountain. Brett noted that there were tax liens outstanding against Meadow Mountain, which if the sale failed, could lose its property in a tax sale, leaving the investors empty handed.

While this deal did not go through, Porter Nelson did not give up on the Meadow Mountain Mining Co. At the end of 1925-beginning of 1926, he wrote to Victor Brett in Bangor, Maine about a director's meeting to be held in Aspen on January 25 to consider a proposal to sell the Company to an unidentified buyer for the sum of $10,000. If this went through, Nelson wanted $5,000 from which he would pay $1,000 to those individuals who had each advanced $100 to pay off the tax liens on the company's property, and also to buy up all outstanding stock of the company at a price of 5 cents per share. Nelson told Brett that he thought many would be happy to sell out at that price. But few did; the Meadow Mountain properties were among the many in the Crystal area that Nelson was trying to sell in 1940.

Porter Nelson was not the only family member to take a fling at mining. On April 22, 1900, his wife Julia Henry bought an undivided 1/8 interest in the Twilight lode mining claim in the Quartz Creek Mining District of Gunnison County. She bought this interest from M. C. McNichols, an Aspen political figure. On January 6, 1906, Julia Henry bought another undivided 1/4 interest in the Jesse lode (as the Twilight lode was then called). She bought this share from a Ms. S. E. Henney, through M. C. McNichols, the attorney for Ms. Henney. On Feb. 11, 1908, Julia bought another 1/4 interest in the Jesse lode. McNichols again was the legal representative for Mrs. Henney. The remaining interest in the Jesse claim was owned by the Raymond Consolidated Mines Co., which had many holdings in Gunnison County. Julia Henry and the Raymond Company filed the necessary applications perfect their claim, which involved having the claim examined by the Forest Service. The ranger who examined the site in July, 1906 reported a scattered tree cover, which he estimated amounted to only 1,000 board feet per acre. He also found evidence that ore had been removed from the spot. On September 17, 1906, the Register of the General Land Office branch at Gunnison, Colorado acknowledged receiving the application for a patent on the Jesse lode mining claim covering 6.461 acres. The Register set the price for this amount of land at $35, or slightly more than $5 per acre. Mineral Certificate No.

800, issued in the name of President Theodore Roosevelt on December 31, 1906, conveyed rights to the Jesse lode to Julia Henry and the Raymond Consolidated Mines Co. There is no evidence that the Jesse lode ever produced much profit for the patent holders.

11

Let the Desert Bloom

The 100th Meridian became symbolically important in U.S. history after the Louisiana Purchase of 1803 brought the United States land lying west of that meridian. The 100th meridian was singled out in the U.S.-Spanish treaty of 1819 as constituting a portion of the boundary between American and Spanish territory in the West. The meridian for a period was considered the boundary between the settled East and the unknown West, west of which, between 1861 and 1869, Congress created a number of new territories to fill the void. And the 100th Meridian was taken as the westernmost boundary of lands where normal agricultural practices were possible. West of that meridian, rainfall was too sparse, the land thus too arid for agriculture as practiced in the wetter East. But Congress early on tackled the problem by passing the Desert Lands Act.[1] This Act, signed into law on March 3, 1877, was aimed at encouraging private persons to bring water to many millions of acres of otherwise useless lands and to cultivate these. Surprisingly, Colorado, which had become a state in 1876, was excluded from this 1877 legislation, although it was clearly in the dry area west of the 100th Meridian. How did Colorado's representatives in Washington allow this to happen?

This omission was corrected in the Timber Culture Repeal Act of March 3, 1891,[2] which made many changes affecting public lands. This 1891 law sensibly recognized that often a group of people, working together, were needed to construct expensive irrigation works. This 1891 law did reduce to 320 acres the maximum area any one person could claim, but on the other hand, helped a claimant by reducing the proportion of land claimed to which he must bring water within the limited time allowed. The opening in 1882 of the 15 million acre Ute reservation in southwest Colorado created new possibilities for Coloradans, even though no free land was available there under the Homestead Act. The law opening the reservation specified that Ute land could only be sold, at a minimum price of $1.25 an acre.

---

1.   19 Stat. 377
2.   26 Stat.1095

Sale of the land would help the government raise the money promised to the Indians for giving up their land. After the White River and Tabeguache Utes were moved out in 1881, and the Ute reservation formally opened to whites in 1892, miners flocked to the mountains; the wetter valleys of the reservation drew the first farmers. A number of Aspen residents in time came to seek arid land on Delta County's Grand View Mesa.

Perhaps the first attempt to obtain land on Grand View Mesa under the Desert Lands Act came on May 26, 1888, five years after Delta County itself was established. On that date, one Eliza S. Zimmerman applied under the Desert Lands Act for 160 acres in section 13 of township 15 south, range 92 West, paying the minimum price of $1.25 per acre. The first of the many Aspen residents to seek land on Grand View Mesa was City Engineer George C. Vickery, who applied for land in section 30 of township 15 South, range 92 West on November 23, 1896. Sarah J. Vickery, George's wife, applied for 320 acres on June 4, 1900 in section 24, township 15 South, range 93 West. Another Aspenite to seek Grand View Mesa land early on was Arthur J. Ingham, who on June 12, 1900 got 240 acres in section 24 of that township. Henry E. Woodward got 160 acres in section 31 of that township on March 14, 1902. Harold W. Clark, a friend of Porter Nelson's from Aspen who went with Nelson in 1898 on a bicycle trip of several hundred miles, got 161.69 acres on April 30, 1902. His purchase was a real bargain, costing him only 25 cents per acre; a 1901 law had eliminated the $1.25 per acre minimum price of former Ute reservation land. Money to pay the Utes was now coming from general revenues, not land sales.

Even the family of Aspen's home capitalist, David R. C. Brown, joined the rush to acquire former Ute reservation land. In 1910, Brown and his second wife Ruth McNutt Brown each applied for 320 acres under the Desert Lands Act, entries nos. 05523 and 05524 at the Montrose branch of the General Land Office. Each stated that the necessary irrigation water would be brought to their tracts through the so-called Scenic Ditch. The Scenic Ditch was a Brown family company; David's younger brother George was President and David's still younger brother Harry was Secretary of that company. David Brown had advanced $20,000 towards construction of this ditch, but Land Office inspectors doubted that the Scenic Ditch could supply the needed water until the Fruitland Irrigation Company had completed and filled its reservoir.[3]

---

3. This reservoir is now usually called the Gould Reservoir. The Brown applications were approved despite the doubts about the Scenic Ditch, because the Browns owned enough shares in the Grand View Canal and Irrigation Company to entitle them to sufficient water from that source, which could deliver water.

In 1894, a law had been passed which among other things encouraged western states and territories themselves to become active in promoting irrigation and not leave it just to private persons. The sponsor of this provision (Section 4 of the "Act making appropriation for the civil expenses of the government for the fiscal year ending June 30, 1895, and other purposes"),[4] was Senator Carey and this provision came to be known as the Carey Act. Carey's basic idea was to have the Federal Government grant each desert land state one million arid acres for reclaiming, with each state paying the General Land Office $1 per acre for the lands it selected. The Carey Act provisions were relaxed in the appropriation act for 1897.[5] The appropriation act for 1902[6] gave Interior money to carry out surveys of lands which might be claimed by states under the Carey Act. Specific encouragement to Colorado to get involved in irrigation came from an act approved February 24, 1909[7] extending the provisions of Carey Act to desert lands within the former Ute reservation. Yet the Carey Act was largely ineffective, states taking up little acreage under its provisions.

But the most important Congressional action to promote development of arid lands in the West was the passage on June 17, 1902,[8] of an act establishing in the Department of Interior a Bureau of Reclamation charged with undertaking major irrigation projects in the West. Private and state action having been found inadequate, the Federal Government would now take a role in providing irrigation in the West. This law is sometimes called the Newlands Reclamation Act after its main sponsor, Senator Newlands of Nevada. One of the first projects under this law was in Colorado: to divert water from the main branch of the Gunnison River to irrigate the dry lands of the Uncompahgre River Valley in the former Ute reservation. A project of this size and uncertain payoff would never have been undertaken by private enterprise.

The diversion of water from the main branch of the Gunnison River into the Uncompahgre Valley did nothing to bring water to the Grand View Mesa where so many Aspenites had taken up land. That Mesa is no Garden of Eden: the average growing season there is less than 140 days, annual precipitation averages less than 11 inches. So in 1901 before Congress created the Bureau of Reclamation, a dozen men owning land on Grand View Mesa and mostly living in Aspen[9] joined to form, under the laws of Colorado, the Grand View Canal and Irrigation Com-

---

4.   28 Stat. 422.
5.   29 Stat. 434.
6.   31 Stat. 1159.
7.   35 Stat. 644.
8.   32 Stat. 1093.

pany. The company was chartered for 20 years, and would issue 4,375 shares of stock valued at $24 per share. The stated purpose of the company was to construct or purchase ditches, canals or reservoirs for irrigating lands owned by the company or its individual shareholders, using water taken from the Smith Fork of the Gunnison River. The water would be drawn somewhere in the south side of section 31, township 15 South, Range 91 West of the 6th Prime Meridian, but the company at its formation had not determined exactly where it would buy or construct any reservoirs. In a case decided in Colorado's 7th District Court over water rights, that Court recognized March 28, 1895 as the priority date for the water rights of the Grand View Canal Company. The Court in its ruling judged the Grand View Canal capable of carrying up to 75 cubic feet of water per second, to irrigate 1,520 acres of land lower down. The Court ruled that, by virtue of appropriation in the original 1895 construction, the Grand View Canal was entitled to withdraw 40.5 cubic feet per second from the river.[10]

The Grand View Canal Company on February 23, 1906 bought from H. E. Woodward, a Company Director, the Castle Peak Ditch and its six associated reservoirs. These installations were situated south of Grand View Mesa, in the part of Colorado where the cadastral survey is based on the New Mexico Prime Meridian. Much of the Castle Peak system being on National Forest land, the Forest Service in 1912 inspected and reported on its installations: "In reference to the reservoir, ditch and tunnel right-of-way over lands in sections 11, 12, 13 and 14, township 50 N., range 5 ½ W. within the Gunnison National Forest, acquired by the Grand View Canal and Irrigation Company by approval of the map filed by it on November 7, 1907, the supervisor reports the following construction work: one ditch six feet wide at the top, three feet wide at the bottom, two feet deep and approximately 3.87 miles in length; one tunnel from Lake No. 3 into Lake No. 5, 3.5 feet by 6.5 feet, approximately 300 feet long and flumed all the way; a dam at the lower end of Reservoir No. 5, 200 feet long and 15 feet high at the outlet. The work that is yet to be completed consists of dams across the lower ends of Reservoirs 1, 2 and 6, and the tunnel from No. 4 to No. 3. The ditch from Castle Peak to the lakes has not been used for two years, the water from the lakes being turned into a natural water course and emptied out again

---

9.   Incorporators from Aspen included Assayer Alonzo Bardwell, miner Henry Hallburg, jeweler Enique Hunkins, mine manager J. M. B. Parry, dentist John Seltzer, mine superintendent H. E. Woodward, mine foreman A. J. Ingham, and former Aspen City Engineer George Vickery. Vickery had formed the Grand View Ditch Company in 1900 (Delta County Document #17043).

10. Decision No. A-31, handed down by the Water Court Division 4 in Delta.

into the lower country for irrigation purposes."[11] So the Grand View Canal Company in 1906 had bought a still incomplete system.

On March 2, 1906, George Vickery, one of the incorporators of the Grand View Canal Company, deeded to that company the so-called Aspen Ditch,[12] also situated in the part of Colorado governed by the New Mexico Prime Meridian. This Aspen Ditch drew its water from Mud Creek. It is not clear why the Canal Company waited some years to buy up the ditches and reservoirs of controlled by insiders Woodward and Vickery.

The Grand View Canal company was far from the first to tap the waters of Smith Fork. A July 2004 tabulation of water rights in the Gunnison River drainage lists a McNeil Ditch as the first to tap Smith Fork water, being credited with water rights dating from April 14, 1882. This date is an anomaly; the Act of Congress opening up the lands of the Ute reservation to whites came into effect only on July 28, 1882.[13] The next earliest date of Smith Fork water rights is February 4, 1883, for the Preston Ditch. These ditches were only small water users. The problem remained: little water ran in Smith Fork after early July.

Perhaps Porter Nelson feared to make desert lands investments in his own name after the turn of the century, just as he did with mining investments. For whatever reason, the Nelson family's first investment in Grand View Mesa land was made in Julia Henry's name. In December, 1904, she took a 50 percent share in 161 acres of land on Grand View Mesa being sold by Aspen attorney and Nelson friend, Harold Clark. Julia Henry's purchase was not a long term investment. She sold her 50 percent share in April, 1909 to the other 50 percent stake holder, Mary V. Clark, Harold's wife. Estate planning?

The year 1909 brought many changes on Grand View Mesa. For one thing, not long after Julia Henry sold the Clark land, Porter Nelson first got his own property there. He did not take this land from the public domain under the Desert Lands Act, but got it from someone who had done so before him (former Aspenite Sarah Vickery). Nelson's main holding was 440 acres in section 24 of township 15 South, Range 93 West, but he also owned 80 adjoining acres at the north border of section 25. The other 80 acres he owned, in section 29 of township 15 S, Range 92 W, had been bought out of the public domain by Asa Simpson in 1900. Nelson did not intend to live on this land, which he came to call his

---

11.   Letter, A. F. Potter, Associate Forrester, to the General Land Office, December 9, 1912. NARA Record Group 49, entry 569, Box 49.

12.   This ditch is not to be confused with the Aspen Ditch furnishing water to the town of Aspen, drawing from another Castle Creek.

13.   21 Stat. 178.

"ranch," but he did go there many times over the years. In a letter written about 1920, he described his Grand View Mesa land this way: "About 20 acres was once in orchard and has been allowed to die. It is now in sage brush. The alfalfa in 1919 cut as follows: first cutting—rick 49 feet long and 14 feet wide; second cutting—51 feet long and 14 feet wide; third cutting got wet a couple of times and was not stacked but fed to sheep from the shock as there was an early snow in October which covered the vegetation. There is a three room shingle roof house made of sawn logs, an excuse for a barn but good enough for summertime, a rock-walled root cellar, and a cistern which needs cleaning and re-cementing." All acceptable to an absentee landlord.

In 1909, the same year that he acquired the ranch on Grand View Mesa, Porter Nelson joined in two efforts organized by W. E. Bates of the Bates Investment Company in Denver's Coronado Building. One Bates' project aimed at selling Grand View land to others, touting the land as fine for growing tree fruit (peaches and especially apples). To this end, Bates formed the Grand View Mesa Land and Orchard Company to which Nelson gave support. Bates' other enterprise was the Grand View Reservoir and Canal Company, formed to buy the assets of Grand View Canal and Irrigation Company and to own mesa land. All these assets would go into a Grand View Irrigation District, which Bates hoped could float bonds to build a reservoir extending the supply of water on Grand View Mesa well into summer and early fall.[14] Porter Nelson joined this second Bates project in a big way, working hard to persuade other land owners on the Mesa to put their land into the new irrigation district. An example of Nelson's work: On June 5, 1909, he got Dora Barnes to sell him an option to purchase her 508 shares of stock in the Grand View Canal and Irrigation Company, and her 320 acres on the Mesa, all for $24,000. Barnes gave Nelson a month to come up with the $1,000 option price, which she agreed would be counted against the final sum due if the option were exercised. Payment of the remaining $23,000 was due only 60 days after the formation and validation of the irrigation district. Barnes also agreed to support the formation of the irrigation district. This deed showed Nelson working at his specialty: getting something done with only minimal capital outlay. Neither Bates' company succeeded.

---

14. The irrigation district, of which W. E. Bates was president and George C. Vickery was secretary, hoped to sell $382,500 worth of bonds, per Delta Deed Book 94, page 38. This sum exceeds the stated $105,000 capitalization of the Grand View Canal and Irrigation Company when formed, and the $218,000 capitalization of the successor company formed in 1922.

The fate of this second Bates' effort was outlined by Porter Nelson's son Carmer in his 1914 application for an extension of time to bring water to land he sought on Grand View Mesa.[15] Carmer said that the irrigation district bonds, although backed by ownership of Grand View Mesa land, found no buyers. The irrigation district was then deemed a failure and annulled. The situation reverted to the *status quo ante*: the Grand View Canal and Irrigation Company, with all its limitations, was the only game on Grand View Mesa for those wanting irrigation water.

Around 1909, Porter Nelson, drawing on his experience as secretary of several mining companies, must have taken over the job as secretary of the Grand View Canal Company.

Nelson was residing in Denver from about 1911 on, but the Grand View Canal and Irrigation Company had an office and a resident manager in the town of Hotchkiss, at least in 1911.[16] Presumably Nelson as Secretary played a role in the adjudication in 1914 in the court in Delta which accorded the Canal and Irrigation Company rights to water from Smith Fork dating from March 28, 1895. Handwritten notes that Nelson kept of a meeting of Canal company shareholders on March 14, 1923 showed him as a major shareholder, with 742 shares of stock, far more than he needed to assure water supply for his own land holdings. The D. W. McIntyre who presided over that meeting held only 280 shares, and a D. W. McIntyre Jr. held 280 shares and an S. J. McIntyre held 280 shares. Nelson's notes show that those attending the 1923 meeting represented a total of 3,012 shares. In January, 1926 Nelson had to postpone a scheduled meeting in Aspen of the Meadow Mountain Mining Company shareholders so that he, as Canal Company Secretary, could attend an adjudication of water rights on the Western Slope arising from California's claim to more water from the Colorado River.

During the Depression, the Grand View Canal Company ran into hard times. As Secretary, Nelson on November 9, 1932 informed David Brown's Aspen State Bank that the Company had no money to pay a note due on November 18th. He told the Bank that "requests have been made on those delinquent in water assessments, but to date, beyond promises to attend soon, no response has been had. Since last May, no money has been paid to the company. In addition to what we owe you, we owe about $70 for labor on the new flume put in the Aspen Ditch last spring. We have paid out this year $150 to you on principal, $200 in interest,

---

15.   More later on Carmer Nelson's Desert Lands Act application.

16.   The Hotchkiss Directory for 1911 shows W. C. Copeland as Canal Company manager. W. C. Copeland was also listed as a physician in Hotchkiss.

taxes $61.67, and for the new flume and work on ditches, $679.69, making a total of $991.36." Nelson's records also show that in December, 1932, he obtained for the company a loan from the Crawford State Bank by mortgaging company property. Was the Crawford bank more sympathetic than the Aspen bank? Hard times lasted well into 1935, when Nelson applied to the Irrigation and Drainage Division of the Reconstruction Finance Corporation for a low interest loan, which he thought would allow the Grand View Canal Company to reduce by some 30% the charges it levied on its customers.

In the summer of 1909, Porter Nelson's son Carmer came for the first time to the Grand View Mesa area to work. He was enthusiastic, saying Hotchkiss "had a great future." In a July 14, 1909 letter to his father, Carmer referred to the newly acquired "our ranch," wrote: "I spent this morning and Monday morning looking over our ranch. I went over the young orchard (apparently in apples) very carefully and found but one tree absolutely dead." Another orchard had peach trees, Carmer writing in the same letter: "I also looked over the peach orchard. I could find but half a dozen trees which have a full crop." A neighbor Carmer called Barnes said that the Nelson trees had been "winter killed." Carmer added that area residents warned against irrigating an orchard on Grand View Mesa after the 10th of August, because this kept the trees growing too late. These people maintained that trees there needed "to season" before the frost set in. The Barnes here was probably the husband of the Dora Barnes who is recorded as buying 320 acres in 1900 in section 25 just south of the Nelson land. Carmer wrote that this Barnes told him that Pete, the man hired to tend the Nelson ranch, had indeed irrigated the orchard late the previous fall. In an August 28 letter, Carmer mentioned two kinds of peaches in the Nelson orchard: early Crawfords, which he called "delicious," and Elbertas. The latter he wrote were small and likely to be frosted before they became ripe. These references pointed to the dangers from the area's short growing season. Grand View Mesa may have indeed produced some fine tree fruit on occasion, but more typically early frosts killed off a year's harvest. In years when this did not happen, the harvests from the over one mile high Grand View Mesa reached a market already sated with fruit harvested earlier from the lower orchards on the north side of the North Fork River. Peach cultivation on Grand View Mesa died out as a result.

The man Carmer called Pete who was running the Nelson ranch in 1909 probably was Peter Christian, one of the early arrivals on Grand View Mesa. General Land Office records show that a Peter Christian in 1912 took over land in section 19, township 15 South, range 92 West when George C. Vickery relinquished it. Peter Christian attended the March 1923 meeting of shareholders in the Grand View Canal Company, holding 160 shares of stock. This Pete was still taking care of the Nelson land in the summer of 1910. In 1911, a man called Pacheco was taking care of the Nelson ranch. This was probably the Saul Pacheco who, according the General Land Office records, got land from the public domain on July 1, 1911 in section 30 of township 15 South, Range 92 West.

Carmer Nelson came back to work on the Grand View Mesa in the summer of 1910. When an employee of the Canal Company quit early that summer, Carmer was hired to patrol the ditches to look for leaks or washouts. While walking the ditches, he saw some Mesa land that interested him. In an August 16, 1910 letter, he asked his father to send him a township map, so he could determine whether anyone had filed on that tract. The next year, he wrote his father: "It certainly looks like a wise move to locate that 160 south of Barnes. What has been done about the water over there? Last year was an exceptionally dry year and was bad for us. We will probably never have that scarcity again, yet we ought to have a sound hold on all the water we can, for without it, the land is practically valueless." More later on Nelson attempts to get land on Grand View Mesa.

Other letters Carmer wrote to his father from Grand View Mesa in the summer of 1910 show how little capacity the Canal Company had to store water. Carmer wrote his father on August 10 as follows: "We opened our reservoir on the 17th of July and have had a constant flow since then. It is nearly out now." This suggests that the reservoir could hold only about 25 days water supply.[17]

Undeterred by the tribulations of those trying to bring water to Grand View Mesa, Julia Henry Nelson on October 5, 1909, filed at the Land Office in Montrose an application under the Deserts Lands Act for 160 acres of Grand View Mesa land. The tracts she applied for were N ½ NE 1/4 of section 13 of township 15 South, range 93 West; and N ½ NW 1/4, W ½ NE 1/4, N ½ SE 1/4 of section 18, township 15 South, range 92 West. While on Grand View Mesa in the summer of 1911, Carmer checked on the status of this land sought by his mother. On August 1, he sent her a tracing of the tract which he said showed that someone named Pierce was infringing on it. Land Office records show that a William H. Pierce applied for 120 acres in section 6 of township 15 South, range 92 West on May 23, 1910. Pierce gave up this filing in May, 1913.

The original Desert Lands Act had given an applicant just 3 years to show that he had brought water to the land applied for. Julia Henry invested $1,000 in stock of the Grand View Canal and Irrigation Company to show how she planned to get the water necessary to cultivate the acres she sought, but that com-

---

17.   This reservoir was probably the Grand View Reservoir built in 1907.

pany by 1913 had not been able to bring water to her land. Because of this delay in the work of the Grand View Company, Julia Henry in September, 1913 applied to the General Land Office for another three years to perfect her claim to the land. A law passed in 1908[18] had given Interior discretion to grant an applicant who, through no fault of his own, had been unable to bring water to his land within the prescribed three years another three years to do so. The General Land Office in April, 1914 decided to gave her just two more years, up to October 5, 1916. She did not learn of on this decision for some time. The Montrose branch was still using her Aspen address, valid when she first applied, and not the Grant Street address in Denver from which she had applied for the extension. The Montrose branch finally in October notified Julia Henry of her extension, using her Denver address.

Now another complication arose with her application. The General Land Office required a married woman applying for land under the Desert Lands Act to show the date of her marriage and that she was not married to a foreigner. This because a 1907 law provided that an American woman marrying a foreigner would lose her citizenship and take on that of her husband, while the Desert Lands Act allowed only American citizens to apply for land. Since Julia Henry had married in 1888 a native-born American (Porter Nelson), she was able to overcome this complication simply by presenting documents to that effect. General Land Office records show that Julia Henry's Desert Lands application was terminated in February, 1915 for failure to show by then that water had been brought to the tract.

Perhaps it was just as well that she did not succeed with her application. A 1995 Bureau of Land Management (BLM) map of the area shows that the tract Julia Henry applied for in 1909 under the Desert Lands Act still was part of the public domain. General Land Office records show that a Harley E. Hutcheson on April 24, 1924 got a permit under the Mineral Leasing Act of February 25, 1920[19] to explore for gas in a wide area which included Julia's claim. But nothing seems to have come of that, and evidently no one else has thought the tract worth trying for.

Julia Henry was not the last Nelson to apply for Grand View Mesa land under the Desert Lands Act. On July 18, 1911 at 11 a.m., James C. Nelson (the full name of Porter's son Carmer), then a college student residing at 1020 15th Street in Boulder, made a declaration at the General Land Office branch in Montrose,

---

18.   34 Stat. 1228.
19.   41 Stat. 437.

Colorado of intent to reclaim 160 acres of land on Grand View Mesa under the act. This was the same tract Carmer had written to his father about earlier. Porter Nelson had filed on it earlier to hold it until his son could apply. Carmer's 1911 application stated that he would obtain water for the tract through the Grand View Canal Company, and that to this end, he had bought shares in the company. Some tense moments for Carmer in filing his claim.

In a July 16, 1911 letter to his father, Carmer told how on the train going to Grand Junction for work on Grand View Mesa, he had met a young woman from Aspen, Henrietta Holthower. He learned that she too was going to Delta to seek land from the public domain, and that she was working with Emmet Gould, a member of a family of Aspen store owners. Young Nelson got the impression that the young lady was thinking of making a claim under the Homestead Act, the provisions of which had been extended to the lands of the former Ute reservation by law on December 13, 1902.[20] Although this was not the case, Carmer feared that she might be going after the very tract that he wanted. In a subsequent letter to his father, Carmer related how the George Vickery's, the former Aspen residents who were helping him with his Desert Land application, were unavailable in Delta until about 3 P.M.. When they showed up, they told him that the map he had prepared of the tract for which he would apply was defective because it did not show the head gate through which water would come to his land. He could not leave for the Land Office in Montrose until a new map had been prepared. Carmer then learned that the lady from the train, whom he thought might be seeking the same tract, had already left Delta in a car with Emmet Gould. Fearing that she might beat him to the Land Office in Montrose, Carmer Nelson found a boy with a "runabout" who agreed to take him from Delta to Montrose and back at a cost of $6. He was pleased, when he reached Montrose on July 18 to learn that not Henrietta nor anyone else had beaten him to the Land Office with an application for the tract of land that he was seeking: the south half of the northwest quarter, and the south half of the northeast quarter of section 25, township 15 South, range 93 West. Records of the General Land Office show that Henrietta Holthower did file an application, for 240 acres of land in section 25, township 15 South, range 93 West on July 22, 1911, well after Carmer and on a different tract. The records show her application was cancelled on December 4, 1913.

So Carmer beat Henrietta and Emmet Gould to the Land Office in Montrose, but Gould was involved in various land matters in the area. Emmet helped the

---

20.   32 Stat. 384.

David Browns with their Desert Lands Act applications. Emmet and his brothers Jim, John, and George had decided to develop a water supply for land on Fruitland Mesa, which rises above the left bank of the Smith Fork of the Gunnison river. Their reservoir was to tap excess spring runoff from Crystal Creek, storing it until needed during the summer. It took three spring runoffs for the Goulds to fill their reservoir to the dam's height of 45 feet (later the height of the dam was raised to 60 feet). The Gould family never made money on their reservoir project. Naming the high mesa to be served by the reservoir "Fruitland Mesa" was rank optimism. Fruitland Mesa is even higher than the Grand View Mesa, and hence even more at the mercy of late frosts. In years of low snowfall, the Gould reservoir could store only 15 or 20 days of irrigation water. The Gould reservoir still operates and appears on maps.

On January 20, 1915, Carmer Nelson appeared again at the Montrose Land Office accompanied by George and Sarah Vickery, this time to apply for an extension of time to prove that an adequate water supply had been brought to his land. His application noted that the Grand View Canal supplies adequate water to the land up to about July 1, but after that he must rely on the Aspen Ditch. This Ditch draws water from Muddy Creek, on which reservoirs exist. The Grand View Canal Company was working to enlarge the Aspen Ditch and its reservoirs, and in a few years was expected to have sufficient water to supply his land. He presented evidence that he had bought 20 shares of stock in the Grand View Canal and Irrigation Company for $500. This was much more than the $1 per acre he was required to expend to bring under cultivation at the required minimum of 20 acres of the 160 for which he was applying. The General Land Office gave Carmer an extension of time up July 21, 1916, making a total of five years after his first application for the land.

Carmer's letters to his father suggest he was of mixed mind about the value of the land he had applied for. In a letter of July 5, 1915, Carmer wrote: "I am tickled to find the eight acres of alfalfa, which I put in, is doing so nicely. What sort of contract did you make with Jordan in regard to my filing? I want to jolly him into breaking as much of that land as possible, without paying him. I won't put a cent into it as I consider the land worth next to nothing. Jordan knows that I have got to prove up on it and also figures that if I don't prove out, he can jump my claim."

When July, 1916 came, Carmer was newly married and managing a farm near Sperryville, Virginia owned by an uncle. From there, Carmer reluctantly abandoned his Desert Lands application. After Carmer abandoned his application, Porter Nelson asked the Land Office branch on Montrose to put the tract up for auction. Montrose turned down this idea, on the grounds that most of the tract was cultivable. Porter Nelson on November 4, 1918 petitioned to have the case re-opened and referred to Washington. On April 5, 1919, Washington authorized sale of the tract, at a price of not less than $10 per acre. On April 14, 1919, the Montrose Land Office branch published a notice in the newspaper _North Fork Times_ stating that offers for the tract would be opened on June 19 at 10 A.M.. Porter Nelson quickly told the Land Office he would not buy the tract at the price of $10 per acre. No other bids were received. In August, 1920, Montrose suggested to the General Land Office in Washington cutting the price to $5 per acre, which Washington approved early in 1922. A notice was published in the paper _Hotchkiss Herald_ on January 17, 1922 stating that offers for the tract would be opened March 14, 1922 at 4 P. M.. Again, no takers. In December, 1946, the Bureau of Land Management (BLM), the successor to the General Land Office, asked Montrose for a report on the status of the 1922 sales authorization. Montrose replied that no sale had been made, and on February 21, 1947 closed its files. It sent Nelson a notice of the file closing, but Nelson had died two months earlier. The tract of land which Carmer and Porter Nelson had sought to claim from the public domain did in time find other takers; a 1995 BLM map shows the tract as privately owned.

Porter Nelson did not look at himself as a rancher or a farmer. In an August, 1942 letter to someone interested in his mining properties around Crystal, Nelson referred to a recent visit to his "ranch," saying "harvest was in full swing, a very interesting season to the landlord." This letter clearly shows Nelson's view of his role, and suggests that whatever arrangement Nelson had with those hired to do the agricultural operations on his property, Nelson probably retained some financial interest in the yield of the land.

Porter Nelson to the end of his life was an officer and mainstay of the irrigation company on Grand View Mesa. On August 3, 1922, after the 1901 articles of incorporation of the Grand View Canal and Irrigation Company had expired, he helped keep Company operations in good legal order. Most of the original 1901 incorporators had been living in Aspen, while by 1921, Aspen was almost a ghost town. Thus only one of the original incorporators could became an incorporator of the successor company: H. E. Woodward, and even he was then living in Denver. Nelson joined with Woodward in forming the successor company, and they brought in Aspen capitalist D. R. C. Brown. Brown's 1910 application for land on Scenic Mesa under the Desert Lands Act had shown that he then owned a significant number of shares of the original Grand View Canal and Irrigation Company. Woodward and Nelson on July 18, 1922 appeared before a notary public in Denver to affix their signatures to the articles of incorporation of the successor company. D. R.. Brown appeared before a notary in Aspen on July 24, 1922 to sign the new incorporation articles.

The new company had a slightly different name from its predecessor: the Grand View Canal Irrigation Company, leaving out the "and." Its main office was to be in Denver, not in Aspen, and its local office was to be in Hotchkiss, not Delta.[21] The new company had a larger capitalization than its predecessor, namely 4,375 shares with the par value of $50. The higher capitalization reflected the fact that the facilities of the renewed company included a small reservoir,[22] the enlarged Daisy Ditch and an extension of the Aspen Ditch serving the reservoir. The stated purposes of the renewed company were more inclusive than those of its predecessor. Not only would the company as before construct and acquire canals, ditches and reservoirs, but would also buy water rights. The company would supply water not only for irrigation of lands owned by the company and by individual members (i. e. shareholders), but also for domestic purposes. The new articles stated specifically that the company was non-profit and "the stock is used as a convenient measure for distribution of water to the stockholders." The company, again, was chartered for 20 years, that is until 1942.

---

21. The old Company had an office in Hotchkiss as early as 1911, a Hotchkiss City Directory of that year showed the Canal Company Manager as residing there.
22. The Grand View Reservoir held only 1545 acre-feet, and was thus smaller than Castle Peak Reservoir No. 1 which held 5606 acre-feet of water.

STATE OF COLORADO,
COUNTY OF....Delta................ } ss.

To Whom It May Concern:

This is to certify that a special meeting of the stockholders of........The..Grand..View............
............Canal..Irrigation..Company..
a Colorado corporation, was held at....Hotchkiss,..Colorado,............on the..31st..day of
......January..............., A. D. 19.42., such meeting having been called by the stockholders representing at least 10 per cent (10%) of the entire capital stock of the company outstanding. Notice of such
meeting, as provided by law, was published *for two successive weeks* at least once not more than thirty days and at least ten days
prior to the date fixed for said meeting in a newspaper printed at....Hotchkiss............................,
State of Colorado, and notice of said meeting was delivered personally or mailed to each stockholder thirty
(30) days prior to the date of such meeting, there being represented at such meeting....3183........
shares of the capital stock of said company out of a total of....4375....................shares outstanding.

At said meeting a resolution was passed to extend the corporate existence of this said corporation*
....making..it..perpetual..............., from and after the date of the expiration of its corporate life,†
the resolution receiving a MAJORITY vote of all the outstanding stock of the corporation. The president
and secretary were authorized to certify this resolution under the corporate seal of the company, to file
such certificate with the Secretary of State of the State of Colorado, and to file duplicate certificate under
seal of the company in the office of the Recorder of Deeds in each county or counties wherein the company may do business in the State of Colorado, and in pursuance of such resolution, we do hereby certify
the same under the seal of the company.

(Corporate Seal)

D.   W.   Mc Intyre   President.

W. Porter Nelson   Secretary.

*Corporate existence may be renewed perpetually or for any specified number of years.
†This certificate of renewal shall be filed before or within one year after the expiration of the charter to be so renewed.
Fee for filing certificate of renewal is $20.00 for $50,000 or less and twenty cents for each additional or fractional part of one thousand dollars of authorized capital stock, plus $5.00 for certificate of renewal.

**Grand View Canal and Irrigation Co.
becomes a permanent company.**

On June 25, 1942, Porter Nelson as Secretary, and D. W. McIntyre as President filed another certificate of incorporation of the Grand View Canal Irrigation Company, this time making it a perpetual corporation. It still operates today.

After Nelson's death, the Federal Government stepped in to address the problem of paucity of water storage capacity along the Smith Fork. Congress approved building storage facilities south of Crawford on April 11, 1956.[23] Construction of the necessary dam began in 1960, with all construction completed in 1962. The Bureau of Reclamation turned over responsibility for operation and maintenance of the Crawford storage project to the Crawford water conservancy district on January 1, 1964. The Crawford Reservoir can hold over 14,000 acre-feet of water, and provides full irrigation service to over 1,400 acres and supplemental irrigation service to 8,056 acres in 131 farms.

The General Land Office in Washington kept a master record of all persons seeking to get land from the public domain under any of the laws which applied, whether the land was mineral, agricultural, timbered, etc. This master record was kept in large bound volumes, with entries made longhand in ink. Colorado Volume No. 72 covered the land on Grand View Mesa. The names of Porter, Julia Henry and James Carmer Nelson were duly entered into that volume following their respective applications under the Desert Lands Act. The volume shows that all their applications came to naught. But they were not alone. Many other persons similarly had high hopes of getting cheap land from the public domain, but in the end were unable to carry through. The Nelson experience in seeking land from the public domain was far from unique.

---

23.   70 Stat. 105.

12

Is the World Running Out of Oil?

Porter Nelson may have been ahead of his compatriots in one sense: during World War I, he invested some time and effort to claim oil shale properties with idea that the world might soon run out of petroleum from wells. In those early years of the 20th century, the motorization age was just dawning. Many then did not realize the coming importance of petroleum. Example: in 1910, the Secretary of the Navy responded negatively to a Senate bill proposing that the U.S. set aside oil-bearing lands still in the public domain to assure the Navy of a sufficient future fuel supply. The Secretary told the Senate that while battleships then under construction were designed to carry about 400 tons of oil, this was only as a reserve fuel for forcing boilers. New torpedo boat destroyers and a few submarines would burn oil exclusively, but the quantity of oil needed by the Navy would be so small as to make unnecessary setting aside the reserves contemplated in the bill. He said that Navy use of oil fuel was unlikely to increase materially. Furthermore, the supply of coal was more general throughout the world than that of oil, and coal was much the safer fuel. He added that the next important advance in the development of power for the Navy would be the adoption of gas engines in place of steam, with that gas to be produced from coal!

World War I changed the views of many regarding the future for oil, in Great Britain first of all. On the eve of World War I, Winston Churchill as First Lord of the Admiralty sponsored a bill in the House of Commons to permit the U. K. Government to buy a large interest in the private Anglo-Persian Oil Company, arguing that this was needed to assure reliable oil supplies for the British Navy. And oil would be needed not just by navies. On Sept. 7, 1914, the commander of French forces fighting against the German attack on Paris mobilized a fleet of Paris taxicabs to carry French reinforcements to the front, arriving in time to halt the German advance. A dramatic demonstration of the value of motorized transport in warfare. World War I saw the British introduce a new weapon, the tank, which required motor fuel. Gasoline-powered aircraft were used in WWI for the first time. All these developments presaged a greatly increased demand for motor fuels.

Even in the United States, fuel supplies became stretched during World War I; motorless Sundays became necessary. In April, 1915, President Wilson moved to secure petroleum reserves for the Navy, as Churchill had done in Britain. Wilson established Naval Petroleum Reserve No. 1 in the Elk Hills area of California, and made a similar designation of a Naval Petroleum Reserve in Wyoming. These were for liquid petroleum. In 1916, Wilson went further, putting into reserves many acres of lands of the Green River oil shale formation. Two Naval Oil Shale Reserves were established in Colorado and one in Utah. In the appropriation act of 1917,[1] the Bureau of Mines was given money to study ways to produce mineral fuels economically, including from shale.

With all these moves focusing on fuel reserves, Porter Nelson went into action. He recorded in the Garfield County, Colorado court house in April, 1917 seven location claims (nos. 56913 to 56919) to lands he described as containing assorted non-hard rock minerals, such as liquid and gaseous hydrocarbons. He cited a 20 year old statute[2] allowing claims for petroleum and other mineral oils to be made under the favorable placer mining provisions of the 1872 mining law. The 1872 law limited to just 20 acres a single person's claim, but no royalties on production were prescribed as happened later. Nelson's 1917 oil shale claims being for 160 acres each, he listed as co-claimants his wife J. H. (Julia Henry) Nelson, his children Carmer, Kate and Marguerite, H. J. Nelson (Carmer's wife), and E. L. Ogden[3] and his wife M. G. Ogden, thus making the eight persons required to claim 160 acres. These 1917 Nelson claims lay south of the Colorado River on Battlement Mesa. This was the area where in the 1970's during Jimmy Carter's Energy Independence program, Exxon started building a new town to provide housing for workers for a planned large oil shale processing project there. The town was later abandoned by Exxon, and subsequently redeveloped by others as housing for retired persons.

Oil was tight in World War II, with gasoline tightly rationed. In addition to the oil shale land claims he personally filed in 1917 for discoveries south of the Colorado River in Mesa and Garfield counties, Porter Nelson during World War

---

1. 39 Stat. 302.
2. 29 Stat. 526.
3. Ed Ogden ran a dry goods store in Aspen, had interests in Grand View Mesa land in Delta County, and like Nelson had mining interests in Crystal. In 1907, Ogden had transferred the Lucky Boy to Nelson, and in 1934, Ogden as trustee had transferred the Inez mine to Nelson.

II acquired from Edward B. McNair some pre-1920 oil shale claims made by others for discoveries lying north of the Colorado River, in Rio Blanco County. These were 22 separate oil shale claims, each for 160 acres, which had been filed in the Rio Blanco County courthouse on Aug. 3, 1918 under the names Sid 1 to 22. The records show that these claims had been located on July 5, 1918 and lay in township 2 South, range 97 West. The various claims were in sections 1, 2 and 3 of that township, also sections 11, 12, 13, 14 and 15, and sections 22 and 23. How these claims passed from the discoverers to Edward B. McNair and then to Porter Nelson is not clear.

These claims were discussed in letters Porter Nelson sent early in 1942 to Charles F. Garlington, his representative in Carbondale, Colorado, asking Garlington to find out if any agricultural entries had been made into the 3,520 acres overlying his Sid shale claims. Garlington could easily go from his Carbondale home to the General Land Office branch in Glenwood Springs, and no doubt had good contacts there who would answer the question at little or no cost to Nelson. BLM records do show that several grazing act patents for some of the land overlying the Sid claims had in fact been granted before 1942. One for 320 acres to Colin R. Maudslay in 1926, a second to Maudslay in 1931 for 313 acres, one to John E. Watkins in 1929 for 167 acres, and one to Donald C. Reed in 1939 for 640 acres. The issuance of these grazing patents in no way invalidated Nelson's pre-existing Sid oil shale claims; mineral rights and surface rights are independent of one another. In 1916, when Congress enacted a law designed to expand grazing[4] and permitted stock-grazing homesteads of up to 640 acres, it specified that these grazing rights did not convey title to any underlying mineral deposits.

The 1920 Mineral Leasing Act[5] ended the patenting under the 1872 Mining Law of claims to land containing coal, phosphate, oil, oil shale, gas or sodium, and imposed a royalty fee for such minerals extracted from public land. The 1920 act grandfathered valid claims to such minerals existing as of January 1, 1919, making old claims like Porter Nelson's more valuable. In 1952, six years after Porter Nelson's death, his son Carmer packaged the seven pre-1920 oil shale claims in Garfield and Mesa Counties with similar adjoining and partially overlapping larger claims owned by a Nettie Cornwall of Denver for the purpose of selling this larger package to the Gulf Oil Co. Gulf Oil agreed to pay the claim owners a fee for the right to explore their holdings. In return, the holders under-

---

4.   39 Stat. 862.
5.   41 Stat. 437.

took to help Gulf Oil obtain patents on the claims, if Gulf decided to buy them. Fortunately for the Porter Nelson heirs who profited therefrom, Gulf Oil did complete the purchase. No oil company bought up the Sid claims, not even during President Jimmy Carter's Energy Independence Program of the late 1970's. The Sid claims were remote from rail transportation routes and lacked the water resources which existed along the Colorado River, and thus did not attract the same interest.

The 1872 Mining Act required a claimant to mineral finds, including oil shale, to perform $100 worth of "assessment work" each year to show that he had not abandoned his claim. During World War II when all manpower was needed for the war effort, Congress suspended this "assessment work" requirement.[6] Instead, a claimant could simply file an affidavit of non-abandonment. BLM records show that Porter's son Carmer filed these affidavits after Porter's death. After Carmer Nelson's own death, a Porter Nelson grandson living in Denver, took over the job of filing the non-abandonment affidavits. In November 1986, the Bureau of Land Management cancelled the Sid claims, the grandson having failed to file, on time, the declaration of intent to maintain them. This was an oversight rather than a conscious decision.

The grandson in a 1987 letter explained to the other heirs what had happened: "You will recall that grandfather at the time of his death had several oil shale and mining claims on the Western Slope. The best of these were patented (sic) oil shale claims which were sold by my Dad some years ago, and the proceeds were distributed to the heirs at that time in accordance with the provisions of grandfather's will.

"Remaining were some unpatented oil shale claims. Grandfather had worked on these over the years, and presumably they were valid. They were regarded by grandfather as of questionable, if any, value, and were put in a trust created by grandfather in conjunction with his will. No further 'assessment work' was ever done on this property but notices of 'intent to hold' were filed with the Department of Interior every year until 1985 when I missed the filing date. When I received a notice from the Department of Interior voiding the claims, I engaged the law firm of Davis, Graham and Stubbs, to investigate the matter as to possible remedies.

"After a thorough investigation, Davis, Graham and Stubbs reported that for the past 30 years, the claims have been invalid because the Deputy Solicitor of the Department of the Interior had determined on April 26, 1957 that the claims

6.   57 Stat. 74.

were void because grandfather had never discovered a 'valuable mineral deposit within the claims.' Davis, Graham and Stubbs state that 'given these circumstances, we believe that further legal action involving the claims would be futile. The 1957 Department of Interior position is virtually unassailable in the light of the failure to pursue judicial remedies for nearly 30 years. Accordingly we do not recommend that you pursue further legal avenues."

The grandson, noting the poor prospects for oil in 1987, said that he was happy the family had not been putting money into assessment work all those years. The government evidently did not see much value in oil reserves then. In 1997, the Department of Energy transferred management of Naval Oil Shale Reserve Tracts 2 and 3 at the base of the Book Cliffs in Colorado to the BLM Glenwood Springs field office for public leasing. President Clinton's Energy Secretary Bill Richardson went to the Northern Ute Indian reservation in January, 2000 to announce the U. S. decision to return 80,000 acres of shale lands to the tribe from whom these had been taken in 1916 for Naval Oil Shale Reserve tract No. 3. Considering these U.S. moves to abandon oil reserves, the voiding of the Sid claims looked like no big deal.

But prospects for oil shale may improve if the price of oil keeps rising. In December, 2004, the Fossil Fuel Branch of the Energy Department published the conclusions of an in-house study of oil shale in the United States. The study noted that Canada was recovering large quantities of oil by mining tar sands in its western provinces. The study proposed that the United States also lessen its dependence on foreign energy by using new technology to extract some of the estimated 2 trillion barrels of recoverable oil held in the oil shale formations in the western United States. Considerable work and government-industry cooperation would of course be required, but with some diehards in the Bush Administration taking up the cudgels for oil shale, perhaps Porter Nelson's Sid oil shale claims might have had a future after all.

The finding of the Denver law firm that Porter Nelson's Sid oil shale claims had been invalidated in 1957 is at odds with Interior Department records showing these claims were canceled only on November 7, 1986, and for failure to file an affidavit of intent to maintain them, rather than because no valid mineral had been discovered. Whatever, Porter Nelson's efforts in the Rio Blanco County oil shale areas came to naught.

13

Porter Nelson in Retrospect

Like Chief Ouray, Porter Nelson did travel to Washington from time to time to meet with government officials. Unlike Ouray, Porter Nelson met no Presidents or Secretaries of Interior in Washington. Nelson met with the Bureau of Mines, or perhaps the General Land Office, not the Office of Indian Affairs. Nelson did have a business agreement with a member of the famed Guggenheim family, who among other enterprises ran the large Philadelphia smelter outside Pueblo. Records show Nelson in 1917 gave one L. Guggenheim of Pueblo County a deed for 2/3 of Nelson's Lucky Queen mine on Sheep Mountain outside Crystal. But this L. Guggenheim seems to have been only a minor, remote member of the famous smelting family.[1]

Porter Nelson's obituary in the *Denver Post* of December 25, 1946 was very brief. It called him a "pioneer mining man." Porter Nelson had bought a sizable plot in the Denver's Fairmount Cemetery when his beloved Julia died in 1919. She was interred there. Unlike Ouray, whose remain lie at the Southern Ute Reservation, miles and mountains from Chipeta's tomb at the Ute Museum near Montrose, Porter Nelson's remains were laid next to those of his beloved Julia.

---

1.   The 1910 census shows this Guggenheim as age 35, born in Tennessee. He may have been the son of the 70 year old Swiss-born saloon keeper, Lee Guggenheim, whom the 1900 census shows as living in Murfreesboro, Tennessee. The rich Guggenheim immigrants were also Swiss-born. Porter Nelson's L. Guggenheim may have been in Pueblo to work at the family's Philadelphia Smelter, but biographies of the rich Guggenheim's do not speak of him.

Porter Nelson Gravestone, Denver

A more significant memorial to Porter Nelson were the many mining properties near Crystal that he had nourished through the hard times and still had on
his death. On March 28, 1940 Porter Nelson had enlisted help from a broker in
selling the many Crystal properties he either owned or controlled. These are: 27
lode mining claims in the Black Queen group; the Lead King group, which
included the Meadow Mountain Mining properties; the Sheep Mountain group
of about a dozen claims and its mill, then still intact; the Inez Group of 15
claims; the Lucky Boy group of five properties; the Bon Ton group, consisting in
part of lapsed claims; the Commonwealth Placer of 160 acres; the North Pole
and Shakespeare Group of 18 patented claims and several unpatented claims; and
also the Harris-Fairly Group of three patented claims. He also wanted to sell the
preliminary work he had done toward building an electric power plant on the

Crystal River, and some lots in the town of Crystal. He wanted $60,000 for all. How much thinking, dealing and hoping he had invested in those mining properties. A few of the Nelson mines, e. g. the Lead King, that he tried to sell in 1940 operated after his death, but only sporadically. One property on his 1940 sales list has become well known: the power plant unit of the old Sheep Mountain Mill. The whole mill installation had collapsed sometime after Nelson's death, but the power plant part of it was resurrected and shored up as a Bicentennial Project in 1976. This restored power plant is now one of the most frequently photographed spots in Colorado.

Power Plant of old Sheep Mountain Mill, Crystal

The house at 525 West Hallam where the Nelson family had their best years in Aspen, and which Nelson had to let go for taxes after he quit town is, after considerable upgrading, now worth several million dollars. *Sic transit gloria mundi.*

Epilogue

Chief Ouray and Porter Nelson each had to endure personal tragedies in their lives. Chief Ouray had no children with the beloved Chipeta, his closest companion and adviser throughout his life. He did have one son, born before Chipeta entered his life. That son at a very tender age was captured by hostile tribe and raised as a member of that tribe. Ouray set great store on recovering his son, and enlisted white support in doing so. When Felix Brunot had the son brought to Washington to meet Ouray, the son initially refused to recognize Ouray as his father. Finally the son became reconciled with Ouray, and asked for time to go back to the tribe which had raised him, there to say his goodbyes. But before the son could join Ouray and the Tabeguache, he died. Troubling to any parent to have a child pre-decease him. Porter Nelson, like Ouray, experienced the pain of a child going before him in death. Porter's daughter Kate died in her early 40s, from an ailment, colon cancer, which was not properly diagnosed until it was too late to save her.

Chief Ouray died young, when only in his 40s. Unlike Ouray, Porter Nelson lived a long life, into his 80s.

While Ouray's wife Chipeta outlived Ouray by decades, Porter's wife Julia left Porter a widower for 25 years. In her early 50's, Julia fell and broke her hip. She seemed to be recovering well in the hospital. Then she suffered a sudden relapse, dying within hours, from what the attending doctor on her death certificate called tuberculosis. Modern medicine looking at the etiology would likely to have attributed her sudden death to a pulmonary embolism. But even if Julia's ailment had been properly diagnosed, there was little that the doctors of her day could have done to save her.

Ouray and Porter were both believers in education for the young. Ouray, with no children of his own, encouraged a nephew to put his children in a school run from time to time at the Los Pinos agency, where the wife of the agent was the teacher. Ouray also facilitated the sending of Tabeguache children to the industrial school which the Government had established at Carlisle, Pennsylvania to train Indians in the skills thought necessary if the Indians were to live a settled, nonnomadic life. In 1880, Ouray and Chipeta took a number of Indians to visit the Indian school at Carlisle to encourage other Utes in the value of education for their young. Porter Nelson showed his interest in education by serving several years on the Aspen School Board, including one year as Chairman. Although his finances were shaky at the time, he managed to pay for a college education for each of his three children.

Ouray was a unifying figure for the Colorado Utes; Porter Nelson was the unifying figure for the branches of his descendants living in Missouri, Colorado and California. Ouray and Porter Nelson lived their lives in different periods of Colorado history, under quite different circumstances. I believe the differences mean that their stories, when paired, provide a broader insight into Colorado's past.

This exposition of the lives of Ouray and Nelson has been enriched by the photographs of Ouray and Chipeta from the Prints and Photographs Division of the Library of Congress. First cousin Thomas Nelson Echternach furnished the photograph of the Denver gravestone of Porter and Julia Henry Nelson. Second cousin Greaner Neal was the source of the photograph of the first store and home of Lewis Porter Nelson, as well as of the Borneo Mining Company stock certificate. My thanks to all.

Index

978-0-595-35860-1
0-595-35860-8

Made in the USA
Las Vegas, NV
05 December 2021